# Colorful
# KNIT SOXX

## 26 sock patterns for warm, happy feet

## Kerstin Balke of Stine & Stitch

**STACKPOLE BOOKS**

Guilford, Connecticut

Published by Stackpole Books
An imprint of The Rowman & Littlefield Publishing Group, Inc.
4501 Forbes Blvd., Ste. 200
Lanham, MD 20706
www.stackpolebooks.com

Distributed by NATIONAL BOOK NETWORK
800-462-6420

The original German edition was published as *SoxxBook by Stine & Stitch*.
Copyright © 2017 frechverlag GmbH, Stuttgart, Germany (www.topp-kreativ.de)
This edition is published by arrangement with Claudia Böhme Rights & Literary Agency, Hannover, Germany
(www.agency-boehme.com).

PHOTOGRAPHS: frechverlag GmbH, 70499 Stuttgart; lichtpunkt, Michael Ruder, Stuttgart
PROJECT MANAGEMENT: Franziska Schmidt, Mareike Upheber
EDITING: Regina Sidabras, Berlin, Germany
ILLUSTRATIONS: Josy Jones Graphic Design & Illustrationen
LAYOUT: Petra Theilfarth
TRANSLATION: Katharina Sokiran

British Library Cataloguing in Publication Information available

**Library of Congress Cataloging-in-Publication Data available**

Name: Balke, Kerstin, author.
Title: Colorful knit soxx : 26 sock patterns for warm, happy feet / Kerstin Balke of Stine & Stitch.
Description: Guilford, Connecticut : Stackpole Books, [2019]
Identifiers: LCCN 2019019085 | ISBN 9780811737937 (pbk. : alk. paper)
Subjects: LCSH: Knitting. | Knitting--Patterns. | Socks.
Classification: LCC TT825 .B2953 2019 | DDC 746.43/2041--dc23 LC record available at https://lccn.loc.
  gov/2019019085

⊖™ The paper used in this publication meets the minimum requirements of American National Standard for Information Sciences—Permanence of Paper for Printed Library Materials, ANSI/NISO Z39.48-1992.

First Edition

Printed in the United States of America

# Getting started with brights

SOXX #1 .................. 10

SOXX #2 .................. 16

SOXX #3 .................. 22

SOXX #4 .................. 28

SOXX #5 .................. 32

SOXX #6 .................. 38

# Knock your socks off in wearable retro

SOXX #7 .................. 46

SOXX #8 .................. 52

SOXX #9 .................. 58

SOXX #10 .................. 64

SOXX #11 .................. 68

3

# Nature at your feet

SOXX # 12 ............... 76

SOXX # 13 ............... 82

SOXX # 14 ............... 86

SOXX # 15 ............... 90

# Anchors aweigh!

SOXX # 16 ............... 98

SOXX # 17 ............... 104

SOXX # 18 ............... 108

SOXX # 19 ............... 112

## Muted hues for putting your feet up

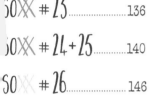

SOXX # 20 ............... 120

SOXX # 21 ............... 126

SOXX # 22 ............... 130

SOXX # 23 ............... 136

SOXX # 24+25 ......... 140

SOXX # 26 ............... 146

## Getting creative with sock design

DESIGN YOUR OWN SOCKS ....................................... 154

## Sock basics

MATERIALS ........................................................ 166

KNITTING BASICS ............................................... 168

THE SOCK ........................................................ 174

ACKNOWLEDGMENTS ........................................ 192

TECHNIQUE INDEX .......................................... 192

# Knitting socks goes everywhere!

Arm yourself with just a DPN set and two or three skeins of yarn and you can get a sock under way in any place—these will fit into any luggage! Handknit socks are nearly indispensable in the colder season and make for a much-appreciated gift.

In this book, you will find a variety of designs, different color variations, and important basic instructions. The colorwork patterns can be worked in sizes Women's 5½ to Men's 11, and even larger than that. Everything you need to know to make them can be found in the chapter "The Sock" on page 174.

If you don't feel ready to venture into stranded knitting with two colors right now, start with striped socks for the time being, and later continue with small colorwork patterns.

*Kerstin Balke*

Getting started

with brights >>>>>>>>>

# SOXX No. 1

## DIFFICULTY LEVEL 3

## SIZES

Women's 5½–Men's 11

Pattern instructions as given are for size Women's 7/8; changes to stitch counts and variations needed for the other sizes are given on page 15.

## YARN AND NEEDLES

Lang Yarns Jawoll; #1 fingering weight yarn; 75% wool, 25% nylon; 230 yd. / 210 m, 1.75 oz. / 50 g per skein; 1 skein each in #94 Off-White, #159 Tangerine, #279 Turquoise, and #116 Kiwi

DPN set of 5 needles in size US 1.5–2.5 / 2.5–3.0 mm

## GAUGE

In stranded pattern on US 1.5–2.5 / 2.5–3.0 mm needles 34 sts and 42 rnds = 4 × 4 in. / 10 × 10 cm

GETTING STARTED WITH BRIGHTS

## Stockinette Stitch

In rows: Knit on RS, purl on WS.
In rnds: Knit all sts in all rnds.

## Cuff Ribbing

Alternate "k1, p1."

## Stranded Patterns A–D

Stitch count has to be a multiple of 4.
Work all rnds in St st from the appropriate
colorwork chart. Repeat the pattern repeat
(4 sts wide) around.

### Colorwork Chart A

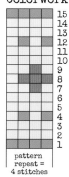

15
14
13
12
11
10
9
8
7
6
5
4
3
2
1

pattern
repeat =
4 stitches

☐ = Kiwi
☐ = Off-White
☐ = Tangerine

### Colorwork Chart B

2
1

pattern
repeat =
4 stitches

☐ = Off-White
☐ = Turquoise

### Colorwork Chart C

4
3
2
1

pattern
repeat =
4 stitches

☐ = Off-White
☐ = Tangerine

### Colorwork Chart D

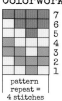

7
6
5
4
3
2
1

pattern
repeat =
4 stitches

☐ = Off-White
☐ = Kiwi
☐ = Tangerine

# INSTRUCTIONS

CO 64 sts in Tangerine, distribute evenly onto 4 DPNs (16 sts per needle), and join into round.

For the cuff, work 13 rnds (1.2 in. / 3 cm) in Cuff Ribbing pattern.

Start the leg in stockinette stitch in stranded pattern A in Kiwi, Off-White, and Tangerine. Work Rnds 1–15 of chart once. Break working yarn in colors Tangerine and Kiwi. Continue in stranded pattern B in Off-White and Turquoise. Work Rnds 1 and 2 of the chart 16 times.

Now, break both yarns and finish the leg with 1 rnd in Kiwi. Break the working yarn.

Work a boomerang heel in stockinette stitch in Kiwi over the 32 sts of Ndls 4 and 1, following instructions on page 183.

Work the foot in stockinette stitch in the round over all sts on all 4 DPNs. Begin with 1 rnd in Kiwi, then break the working yarn.

After this, work in stranded pattern C in Off-White and Tangerine. Work Rnds 1–4 of chart 10 times.

Now, continue in stranded pattern D in Off-White, Kiwi, and Tangerine. Work Rnds 1–7 of the chart once. Break the working yarn in colors Kiwi and Off-White, and finish the foot in Tangerine, starting toe decreases after 6.9 in. / 17.5 cm from middle of heel.

Work toe with paired banded decreases according to instructions on page 189 in Tangerine. Now, break the working yarn, and pull the end through to the inside of the sock.

Weave in all ends.

Work the second sock the same way.

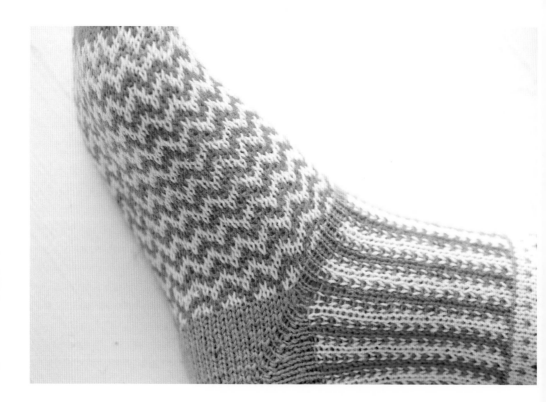

GETTING STARTED WITH BRIGHTS

## STITCH COUNTS AND VARIATIONS FOR OTHER SIZES

### WOMEN'S $5^1/_2$/6
CO 64 sts (16 sts per needle).
Foot, Colorwork Chart C: Work Rnds 1–4 of chart 7 times.
Continue as stated in pattern, starting toe decreases
6.3 in. / 16 cm from middle of heel.

### WOMEN'S 9/$9^1/_2$, MEN'S 7/$7^1/_2$
CO 68 sts (17 sts per needle).
Foot, Colorwork Chart C: Work Rnds 1–4 of chart 10 times.
Continue as stated in pattern, starting toe decreases
7.5 in. / 19 cm from middle of heel.

### WOMEN'S 11/12, MEN'S $8^1/_2$/9
CO 68 sts (17 sts per needle).
Foot, Colorwork Chart C: Work Rnds 1–4 of chart 11 times.
Continue as stated in pattern, starting toe decreases
8.1 in. / 20.5 cm from middle of heel.

### MEN'S 10/11
CO 72 sts (18 sts per needle).
Foot, Colorwork Chart C: Work Rnds 1–4 of chart 12 times.
Continue as stated in pattern, starting toe decreases
8.7 in. / 22 cm from middle of heel.

# SOXX NO. 2

### DIFFICULTY LEVEL 3

### SIZES

Women's 5½–Men's 11

Pattern instructions as given are for size Women's 7/8; changes to stitch counts and variations needed for the other sizes are given on page 20.

### YARN AND NEEDLES

Lang Yarns Jawoll; #1 fingering weight yarn; 75% wool, 25% nylon; 230 yd. / 210 m, 1.75 oz. / 50 g per skein; 1 skein each in #01 White, #159 Tangerine, and #116 Kiwi

DPN set of 5 needles in size US 1.5–2.5 / 2.5–3.0 mm

### GAUGE

In stranded pattern on US 1.5–2.5 / 2.5–3.0 mm needles 32 sts and 42 rnds = 4 × 4 in. / 10 × 10 cm

GETTING STARTED WITH BRIGHTS

## Stockinette Stitch

In rows: Knit on RS, purl on WS.
In rnds: Knit all sts in all rnds.

## Cuff Ribbing

Alternate "k1-tbl, p1."

## Knitting through the Back Loop (tbl)

Insert the needle from right to left into the
back leg of the stitch; knit the stitch this way
so it ends up twisted.

## Colorwork Charts A and B

Stitch count has to be a multiple of 4.
In all rnds, work in stockinette stitch from
appropriate colorwork chart. Repeat the
pattern repeat (4 sts wide) around.

### Colorwork Chart A

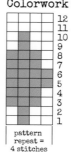

12
11
10
9
8
7
6
5
4
3
2
1

pattern
repeat =
4 stitches

☐ = White
▨ = Kiwi

### Colorwork Chart B

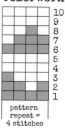

10
9
8
7
6
5
4
3
2
1

pattern
repeat =
4 stitches

▨ = Kiwi
☐ = White

# INSTRUCTIONS

CO 64 sts in Tangerine, distribute evenly onto 4 DPNs (16 sts per needle), and join into round.

For the cuff, work 12 rnds (1.2 in. / 3 cm) in Cuff Ribbing pattern. Break the working yarn, and work the leg, starting with 1 rnd in White. Now, continue in stranded pattern from Chart A in White and Kiwi. Work Rnds 1–12 of the chart 4 times in all. Break working yarn in both colors.

Now, work a boomerang heel in stockinette stitch in Tangerine over the 32 sts of Ndls 4 and 1, following instructions on page 183, then break the working yarn.

Work the foot in stockinette stitch in the round over all sts on all 4 DPNs, starting with 2 rnds in White, then continue in stranded pattern B in Kiwi and White. Work Rnds 1–10 of the chart 5 times, then work only Rnds 1–5 once more. Break working yarn in Kiwi and White, and finish the foot

## STITCH COUNTS AND VARIATIONS FOR OTHER SIZES

**WOMEN'S 5½/6**
CO 64 sts (16 sts per needle).
Foot, Colorwork Chart B: Work Rnds 1–10 of the chart 4
times, then only Rnds 1–5 once. Continue as stated in pattern, starting toe decreases 6.3 in. / 16 cm from middle
of heel.

**WOMEN'S 9/9½, MEN'S 7/7½**
CO 68 sts (17 sts per needle).
Foot, Colorwork Chart B: Work Rnds 1–10 of the chart 6
times. Continue as stated in pattern, starting toe decreases
7.5 in. / 19 cm from middle of heel.

**WOMEN'S 11/12, MEN'S 8½/9**
CO 68 sts (17 sts per needle).
Foot, Colorwork Chart B: Work Rnds 1–10 of the chart 6
times, then only Rnds 1–5 once. Continue as stated in pattern, starting toe decreases 8.1 in. / 20.5 cm from middle
of heel.

**MEN'S 10/11**
CO 72 sts (18 sts per needle).
Foot, Colorwork Chart B: Work Rnds 1–10 of the chart 7 times.
Continue as stated in pattern, starting toe decreases 8.7 in.
/ 22 cm from middle of heel.

in Tangerine. After 6. 9 in. / 17.5 cm from middle of heel, start toe decreases.
Work paired banded toe decreases according to instructions on page 189 in Tangerine.

Break the working yarn, and pull the end through to the inside of the sock.
Weave in all ends.
Work the second sock the same way.

# SOXX no. 3

## SIZES

Women's 5½–Men's 11

Pattern instructions as given are for size Women's 7/8; changes to stitch counts and variations needed for the other sizes are given on page 27.

## YARN AND NEEDLES

Lang Yarns Jawoll; #1 fingering weight yarn; 75% wool, 25% nylon; 230 yd. / 210 m, 1.75 oz. / 50 g per skein; 1 skein each in #22 Light Beige Heathered, #159 Tangerine, #43 Yellow, and #249 Golden Yellow

DPN set of 5 needles in size US 1.5–2.5 / 2.5–3.0 mm

## GAUGE

In stranded pattern on US 1.5–2.5 / 2.5–3.0 mm needles
34 sts and 36 rnds = 4 × 4 in. / 10 × 10 cm

## Stockinette Stitch

In rows: Knit on RS, purl on WS.
In rnds: Knit all sts in all rnds.

## Cuff Ribbing

Alternate "k1, p1."

## Colorwork Charts A–H

Stitch count has to be a multiple of 4.
In all rnds, work in stockinette stitch from appropriate colorwork chart. Repeat the pattern repeat (4 sts wide) around.

# INSTRUCTIONS

CO 64 sts in Light Beige Heathered, evenly distribute onto 4 DPNs (16 sts per needle), and join into round.

For the cuff, work 15 rnds (1.2 in. / 3 cm) in Cuff Ribbing pattern.

Work the leg in stockinette stitch. Start with 2 rnds in Light Beige Heathered, then continue from Colorwork Chart A in Light Beige Heathered and Tangerine. Work Rnds 1–4 of chart once. Now, work Rnds 1–4 of Colorwork Chart B 3 times. Break

### Colorwork Chart A

pattern repeat = 4 stitches

■ = Tangerine
□ = Light Beige Heathered

### Colorwork Chart B

pattern repeat = 4 stitches

□ = Tangerine
■ = Light Beige Heathered

### Colorwork Chart C

pattern repeat = 4 stitches

■ = Golden Yellow
□ = Light Beige Heathered

### Colorwork Chart D

pattern repeat = 4 stitches

□ = Light Beige Heathered
□ = Yellow

### Colorwork Chart E

pattern repeat = 4 stitches

□ = Yellow
□ = Light Beige Heathered

### Colorwork Chart F

pattern repeat = 4 stitches

□ = Light Beige Heathered
■ = Golden Yellow

### Colorwork Chart G

pattern repeat = 4 stitches

■ = Tangerine
□ = Light Beige Heathered

### Colorwork Chart H

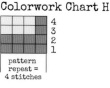

pattern repeat = 4 stitches

■ = Tangerine
□ = Light Beige Heathered

working yarn in Tangerine and work 2 rnds in Light Beige Heathered. Now, continue in Golden Yellow and Light Beige Heathered from Chart C. Work Rnds 1–4 of chart 3 times. Break working yarn in Golden Yellow, and work 2 rnds in Light Beige Heathered. Now, continue in Yellow and Light Beige Heathered from Chart D. Work Rnds 1–4 of chart 3 times. Finish the leg with 1 rnd Light Beige Heathered. Break working yarn in Light Beige Heathered and Yellow.

Now, work a boomerang heel in stockinette stitch in Tangerine over the 32 sts of Ndls 4 and 1, following instructions on page 183. After the first (upper) half of the heel, work 2 rnds over all sts in Light Beige Heathered. Now, break the working yarn, and finish the second (bottom) half of the heel in Tangerine. Break working yarn in Tangerine.

Work the foot in stockinette stitch in the round over all sts on all 4 DPNs. Begin with 1 rnd in Light Beige Heathered. After this, continue in Yellow and Light Beige Heathered from Chart E. Work Rnds 1–4 of chart 3 times. Break working yarn in Yellow, and work 2 rnds in Light Beige Heathered. Now, continue in Golden Yellow and Light Beige Heathered from Chart F. Work Rnds 1–4 of chart 3 times. Break working yarn in Golden Yellow, and work 2 rnds in Light Beige Heathered. Now, continue in Tangerine and Light Beige Heathered from Chart

G. Work Rnds 1–4 of this chart 3 times, then work Rnds 1–4 of Chart H once. Break working yarn in Tangerine, and finish the foot in Light Beige Heathered. After 8 in. / 20 cm from middle of heel, start decreases for the rounded toe.

Work rounded toe according to instructions on page 189. Graft the remaining opening in Kitchener stitch (see page 190).

Weave in all ends.

Work the second sock the same way.

GETTING STARTED WITH BRIGHTS

# STITCH COUNTS AND VARIATIONS FOR OTHER SIZES

**WOMEN'S 5½/6**

CO 64 sts (16 sts per needle).

Foot:

Colorwork chart E: Work Rnds 1-4 of chart 3 times.

Colorwork chart F: Work Rnds 1-4 of chart twice.

Colorwork chart G: Work Rnds 1-4 of chart 3 times.

Continue as stated in pattern, starting decreases for the rounded toe after 7.3 in. / 18.5 cm from middle of heel.


**WOMEN'S 9/9½, MEN'S 7/7½**

CO 68 sts (17 sts per needle).

Foot:

Colorwork chart E: Work Rnds 1-4 of chart 3 times.

Colorwork chart F: Work Rnds 1-4 of chart 4 times.

Colorwork chart G: Work Rnds 1-4 of chart 3 times.

Continue as stated in pattern, starting decreases for the rounded toe after 8.5 in. / 21.5 cm from middle of heel.


**WOMEN'S 11/12, MEN'S 8½/9**

CO 68 sts (17 sts per needle).

Foot:

Colorwork chart E: Work Rnds 1-4 of chart 4 times.

Colorwork chart F: Work Rnds 1-4 of chart 4 times.

Colorwork chart G: Work Rnds 1-4 of chart 4 times.

Continue as stated in pattern, starting decreases for the rounded toe after 9.1 in. / 23 cm from middle of heel.

# SOXX NO. 4

### DIFFICULTY LEVEL 2

### SIZES

Women's 5½–Men's 11

Pattern instructions as given are for size Women's 7/8; changes to stitch counts and variations needed for the other sizes are given on page 31.

### YARN AND NEEDLES

Schoppel ALB Lino; #1 super fine weight yarn 85% lambswool, 15% linen; 438 yd. / 400 m, 3.5 oz. / 100 g per skein; 1 skein in #701 Papaya

DPN set of 5 needles in size US 2.5–6 / 3.0–4.0 mm

### GAUGE

In pattern stitch with passed-over yarn overs on US 2.5–6 / 3.0–4.0 mm needles
28 sts and 38 rnds = 4 × 4 in. / 10 × 10 cm

## Stockinette Stitch

In rows: Knit on RS, purl on WS.
In rnds: Knit all sts in all rnds.

## Knitting through the Back Loop (tbl)

Insert the needle from right to left into the back leg of the stitch; knit the stitch this way so it ends up twisted.

## Pattern with Passed-Over Yarn Overs

Rnd 1: *K2, yo, k2, pass the yo over both sts, rep from * to end of rnd.
Rnds 2 and 3: Knit all sts.
Rnd 4: *Yo, k2, pass the yo over both sts, k2, rep from * to end of rnd.
Rnds 5 and 6: Knit all sts.
Repeat Rnds 1–6.

## Cuff Ribbing

Alternate "k1-tbl, p1."

# INSTRUCTIONS

CO 56 sts, distribute evenly onto 4 DPNs and join into round (14 sts per needle).

For the cuff, work 20 rnds (2.2 in. / 5.5 cm) in Cuff Ribbing pattern.

Begin the leg with 4 rnds in stockinette stitch, then change to textured pattern with passed-over yarn overs. Up to the heel, work Rnds 1–6 of pattern 5 times.

Work turned heel with heel flap in stockinette stitch over the 28 sts of Ndls 4 and 1 according to instructions on page 186.

Work the foot in the round again over all sts of all 4 DPNs. The sts of Ndls 4 and 1 create the sole, which is worked in stockinette stitch to the end. Continue the textured pattern with passed-over yarn overs over the instep (Ndls 2 and 3), making sure that the pattern is stacked evenly. Work Rnds 1–6 a total of 9 times, then work only Rnd 1 once more. Continue in stockinette stitch until a length of 8 in. / 20 cm from middle of heel has been reached. Now, begin decreases for the rounded toe.

Work rounded toe, following instructions on page 189. Graft the remaining opening in Kitchener stitch (see page 190).

Weave in all ends.

Work the second sock the same way.

**WOMEN'S 5½/6**
CO 56 sts (14 sts per needle).
Foot: Work Rnds 1–6 of chart 8 times, then work only Rnd 1 once. Continue as stated in pattern, starting decreases for the rounded toe after 7.3 in. / 18.5 cm from middle of heel.

**WOMEN'S 9/9½, MEN'S 7/7½**
CO 60 sts (15 sts per needle).
Foot: Work Rnds 1–6 of chart 10 times, then work only Rnd 1 once. Continue as stated in pattern, starting decreases for the rounded toe after 8.5 in. / 21.5 cm from middle of heel.

**WOMEN'S 11/12, MEN'S 8½/9**
CO 60 sts (15 sts per needle).
Foot: Work Rnds 1–6 of chart 11 times, then work only Rnd 1 once. Continue as stated in pattern, starting decreases for the rounded toe after 9.1 in. / 23 cm from middle of heel.

**MEN'S 10/11**
CO 64 sts (16 sts per needle).
Foot: Work Rnds 1–6 of chart 11 times, then work only Rnd 1 once. Continue as stated in pattern, starting decreases for the rounded toe after 9.6 in. / 24.5 cm from middle of heel.

# SOXX NO.5

## DIFFICULTY LEVEL 2

## SIZES

Women's 5½–Men's 11

Pattern instructions as given are for size Women's 7/8; changes to stitch counts and variations needed for the other sizes are given on page 37.

## YARN AND NEEDLES

Lang Yarns Jawoll; #1 fingering weight yarn; 75% wool, 25% nylon; 230 yd. / 210 m, 1.75 oz. / 50 g per skein 1 skein each; in #94 Off-White, #159 Tangerine, #279 Turquoise, #43 Yellow, and #116 Kiwi

DPN set of 5 needles in size US 1.5–2.5 / 2.5–3.0 mm

## GAUGE

In stranded pattern on US 1.5–2.5 / 2.5–3.0 mm needles 32 sts and 42 rnds = 4 × 4 in. / 10 × 10 cm

GETTING STARTED WITH BRIGHTS

## Stockinette Stitch

In rows: Knit on RS, purl on WS.
In rnds: Knit all sts in all rnds.

## Cuff Ribbing

Alternate "k1, p1."

## Colorwork Chart

Stitch count has to be a multiple of 4.
Work all rnds in St st from colorwork chart.
Repeat the pattern repeat (4 sts wide) around.
After each colorwork pattern, break the working yarn in that color.

### Colorwork Chart

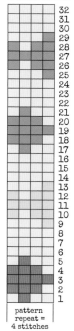

pattern repeat = 4 stitches

☐ = Off-White
▨ = Tangerine
☐ = Yellow
▨ = Turquoise
▨ = Kiwi

# INSTRUCTIONS

CO 64 sts in Kiwi, distribute evenly onto 4 DPNs (16 sts per needle), and join into round.

For the cuff, work 2 rnds in Kiwi and 10 rnds in Off-White in Cuff Ribbing pattern (1.2 in. / 3 cm). Break the working yarn in Kiwi.

Work the leg in stockinette stitch, beginning with 2 rnds in Off-White. Now, continue in stranded pattern in Off-White, Tangerine, Yellow, Turquoise and Kiwi. Work Rnds 1–32 of the chart once, then work only Rnds 1–21 once more.

Now, work a boomerang heel in stockinette stitch in Off-White over the 32 sts of Ndls 4 and 1, following instructions on page 185.

Work the foot in the round over all sts on all 4 DPNs in stranded pattern in Off-White, Kiwi, Tangerine, Yellow, and Turquoise. Work Rnds 24–32 of the chart once, work Rnds 1–32 once, then work only Rnds 1–13 once. After 6.9 in. / 17.5 cm from middle of heel, start toe decreases.

Work toe with paired banded decreases in Off-White, following instructions on page

189. Break the working yarn, and pull the end through to the inside of the sock.
Weave in all ends.
Work the second sock the same way.

GETTING STARTED WITH BRIGHTS

## STITCH COUNTS AND VARIATIONS FOR OTHER SIZES

WOMEN'S 5½/6
CO 64 sts (16 sts per needle).
Foot: Work Rnds 24–32 of chart once, Rnds 1–32 once, then work only Rnds 1–5 once. After 6.3 in. / 16 cm from middle of heel, start toe decreases.

WOMEN'S 9/9½, MEN'S 7/7½
CO 68 sts (17 sts per needle).
Foot: Work Rnds 24–32 of chart once, Rnds 1–32 once, then work only Rnds 1–13 once. After 7.5 in. / 19 cm from middle of heel, start toe decreases.

WOMEN'S 11/12, MEN'S 8½/9
CO 68 sts (17 sts per needle).
Foot: Work Rnds 24–32 of chart once, Rnds 1–32 once, then work only Rnds 1–21 once. After 8.1 in. / 20.5 cm from middle of heel, start toe decreases.

MEN'S 10/11
CO 72 sts (18 sts per needle).
Foot: Work Rnds 24–32 of chart once, Rnds 1–32 once, then work only Rnds 1–29 once. After 8.7 in. / 22 cm from middle of heel, start toe decreases.

# SOXX NO.6

## DIFFICULTY LEVEL 2

## SIZES

Women's 5½–Men's 11

Pattern instructions as given are for size Women's 7/8; changes to stitch counts and variations needed for the other sizes are given on page 43.

## YARN AND NEEDLES

Lang Yarns Jawoll; #1 fingering weight yarn; 75% wool, 25% nylon; 230 yd. / 210 m, 1.75 oz. / 50 g per skein; 1 skein each in #94 Off-White, #249 Golden Yellow, and #116 Kiwi

DPN set of 5 needles in size US 1.5–2.5 / 2.5–3.0 mm

## GAUGE

In stranded pattern on US 1.5–2.5 / 2.5–3.0 mm needles 34 sts and 36 rnds = 4 × 4 in. / 10 × 10 cm

GETTING STARTED WITH BRIGHTS

## Stockinette Stitch

In rows: Knit on RS, purl on WS.
In rnds: Knit all sts in all rnds.

## Knitting through the Back Loop (tbl)

Insert the needle from right to left into the
back leg of the stitch; knit the stitch this way
so it ends up twisted.

## Cuff Ribbing

Alternate "k1-tbl, p1."

## Colorwork Charts A and B

Stitch count has to be a multiple of 4.
Work all rnds in St st from the appropriate
colorwork chart. Repeat the pattern repeat
(4 sts wide) around.

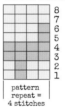

Colorwork Chart A

```
8
7
6
5
4
3
2
1
```
pattern
repeat =
4 stitches

☐ = Off-White
▨ = Golden Yellow

Colorwork Chart B

```
8
7
6
5
4
3
2
1
```
pattern
repeat =
4 stitches

☐ = Off-White
▨ = Kiwi

# INSTRUCTIONS

CO 64 sts in Golden Yellow, distribute evenly onto 4 DPNs (16 sts per needle), and join into round.

For the cuff, work 30 rnds (2.8 in. / 7 cm) in Cuff Ribbing pattern.

Start the leg in stranded pattern A in Off-White and Golden Yellow. Work Rnds 3–8 of the chart once, then Rnds 1–8 twice, then work only Rnds 1–6 once more. Break working yarn in Golden Yellow.

Now, work a boomerang heel in stockinette stitch in Off-White over the 32 sts of Ndls 4 and 1, following instructions on page 183.

Work the foot in stockinette stitch in the round over all sts on all 4 DPNs in stranded pattern B in Off-White and Kiwi. Work Rnds 1–8 of the chart 6 times. Break the working yarn in Kiwi, and continue the foot in Off-White. After 6.9 in. / 17.5 cm from middle of heel, start toe decreases.

Work toe with paired banded decreases according to instructions on page 189 in Off-White, then break the working yarn, and pull the end through to the inside of the sock.

Weave in all ends.
Work the second sock the same way.

GETTING STARTED WITH BRIGHTS

### WOMEN'S 5½/6
CO 64 sts (16 sts per needle).
Foot: Work Rnds 1-8 of Chart B a total of 5 times. After 6.3 in. / 16 cm from middle of heel, start toe decreases.

### WOMEN'S 9/9½, MEN'S 7/7½
CO 68 sts (17 sts per needle).
Foot: Work Rnds 1-8 of Chart B a total of 6 times. After 7.5 in. / 19 cm from middle of heel, start toe decreases.

### WOMEN'S 11/12, MEN'S 8½/9
CO 68 sts (17 sts per needle).
Foot: Work Rnds 1-8 of Chart B a total of 7 times. After 8.1 in. / 20.5 cm from middle of heel, start toe decreases.

### MEN'S 10/11
CO 72 sts (18 sts per needle).
Foot: Work Rnds 1-8 of Chart B a total of 7 times. After 8.7 in. / 22 cm from middle of heel, start toe decreases.

Knock your socks off in

*wearable retro* >>>>>>>>>

# SOXX NO. 7

## DIFFICULTY LEVEL 2

## SIZES

Women's 5½–Men's 11

Pattern instructions as given are for size Women's 7/8; changes to stitch counts and variations needed for the other sizes are given on page 50.

## YARN AND NEEDLES

Schoppel ALB Lino; #1 super fine weight yarn; 438 yd. / 400 m, 3.5 oz. / 100 g per skein; 1 skein in #581 Old Gold

DPN set of 5 needles in size US 2.5–6 / 3.0–4.0 mm

## GAUGE

In Matchstick pattern on US 2.5–6 / 3.0–4.0 mm needles 30 sts and 38 rnds = 4 × 4 in. / 10 × 10 cm

## Stockinette Stitch

In rows: Knit on RS, purl on WS.
In rnds: Knit all sts in all rnds.

## Knitting through the Back Loop (tbl)

Insert the needle from right to left into the back leg of the stitch; knit the stitch this way so it ends up twisted.

## Purling through the Back Loop (tbl)

Insert the needle from left to right into the back leg of the stitch; purl the stitch this way so it ends up twisted.

## Cuff Ribbing

Alternate "k1-tbl, p1."

## Matchstick Pattern

Stitch count has to be a multiple of 4.

Work in the round from the chart or written instructions below. In Rnds 1–5, begin with the 2 sts before the pattern repeat, repeat the pattern repeat (4 sts wide, shaded in chart) around, ending with the 2 sts after the pattern repeat. In Rnds 6–10, repeat the pattern repeat (4 sts wide, shaded in chart) around. Repeat Rnds 1–10.

Rnds 1–5: P2, *k1-tbl, p3, rep from*, ending with "k1-tbl, p1."

Rnds 6–10: *K1-tbl, p3, rep from * to end of rnd.

### Matchstick Pattern Chart

| | | | | | | | | |
|---|---|---|---|---|---|---|---|---|
| – | – | – | ◆ | – | – | – | ◆ | 10 |
| – | – | – | ◆ | – | – | – | ◆ | 9 |
| – | – | – | ◆ | – | – | – | ◆ | 8 |
| – | – | – | ◆ | – | – | – | ◆ | 7 |
| – | – | – | ◆ | – | – | – | ◆ | 6 |
| – | ◆ | – | – | – | ◆ | – | – | 5 |
| – | ◆ | – | – | – | ◆ | – | – | 4 |
| – | ◆ | – | – | – | ◆ | – | – | 3 |
| – | ◆ | – | – | – | ◆ | – | – | 2 |
| – | ◆ | – | – | – | ◆ | – | – | 1 |

– = p1
◆ = k1-tbl

## Heel Pattern

Work in back-and-forth rows with turning, following the chart or written instructions. Repeat Rows 1 and 2.

Row 1 (RS): K3, *p1, k1-tbl, rep from*, ending with "k3."

Row 2 (WS): K3, *p1-tbl, k1, rep from*, ending with "k3."

## Heel Pattern Chart (Ndls 4 and 1)

pattern repeat = 28 stitches

■ = k1
− = p1
◆ = k1-tbl
◇ = p1-tbl

## WOMEN'S 5½/6

CO 56 sts (14 sts per needle)

Foot: Work the instep in Matchstick pattern, work Rnds 1-10 in Matchstick pattern four times, then change pattern to Cuff Ribbing, starting toe decreases 6.3 in. / 16 cm from middle of heel.

## WOMEN'S 9/9½, MEN'S 7/7½

CO 60sts (15 sts per needle).

Foot: Work the instep in Matchstick pattern, work Rnds 1-10 five times, work only Rnds 1-5 once, then change pattern to Cuff Ribbing, starting toe decreases 7.5 in. / 19 cm from middle of heel.

## WOMEN'S 11/12, MEN'S 8½/9

CO 60 sts (15 sts per needle).

Foot: Work the instep in Matchstick pattern, work Rnds 1-10 six times, then change pattern to Cuff Ribbing, starting toe decreases 8.1 in. / 20.5 cm from middle of heel.

## MEN'S 10/11

CO 64 sts (16 sts per needle).

Foot: Work the instep in Matchstick pattern, work Rnds 1-10 six times, then work only Rnds 1-5 once, then change pattern to Cuff Ribbing, starting toe decreases 8.7 in. / 22 cm from middle of heel.

# INSTRUCTIONS

CO 56 sts, distribute evenly onto 4 DPNs (14 sts per needle), and join into round.

For the cuff, work 10 rnds (1.2 in. / 3 cm) in Cuff Ribbing pattern.

Now, work the leg in Matchstick pattern. Work from chart, working Rnds 1–10 a total of 6 times.

Work turned heel with heel flap according to instructions on page 186 and in Heel pattern (see page 49). The heel turn is worked in stockinette stitch.

Work the foot in the round over all sts on all 4 DPNs. Over the sts of Ndls 4 and 1, work the sole to end in stockinette stitch. Over the sts of Ndls 2 and 3, work the instep in Matchstick pattern, working Rnds 1–10 a total of 5 times, and making sure that the pattern is stacked evenly. After this, on the instep only, change pattern to Cuff Ribbing. After 6.9 in. / 17.5 cm from middle of heel, start toe decreases.

Work paired banded toe decreases according to instructions on page 189. Break the working yarn, and pull the end through to the inside of the sock.

Weave in all ends.

Work the second sock the same way.

# SOXX No. 8

### DIFFICULTY LEVEL 3

### SIZES

Women's 5½–Men's 11

Pattern instructions as given are for size Women's 7/8; changes to stitch counts and variations needed for the other sizes are given on page 57.

### YARN AND NEEDLES

Lang Yarns Jawoll; #1 fingering weight yarn; 75% wool, 25% nylon; 230 yd. / 210 m, 1.75 oz. / 50 g per skein; 1 skein each in #94 Off-White, #04 Black, and #150 Gold

DPN set of 5 needles in size US 1.5–2.5 / 2.5–3.0 mm

### GAUGE

In stranded pattern on US 1.5–2.5 / 2.5–3.0 mm needles 32 sts and 40 rnds = 4 × 4 in. / 10 × 10 cm

KNOCK YOUR SOCKS OFF IN WEARABLE RETRO

## Stockinette Stitch

In rows: Knit on RS, purl on WS.
In rnds: Knit all sts in all rnds.

## Cuff Ribbing

Alternate "k1, p1."

## Colorwork Charts A and B

Stitch count has to be a multiple of 4.
Work all rnds in St st from the appropriate
   colorwork chart. Repeat the pattern repeat
   (4 sts wide) around.

### Colorwork Chart A

11
10
9
8
7
6
5
4
3
2
1

pattern
repeat =
4 stitches

■ = Black
□ = Off-White

### Colorwork Chart B

12
11
10
9
8
7
6
5
4
3
2
1

pattern
repeat =
4 stitches

□ = Off-White
▨ = Gold

## INSTRUCTIONS

CO 64 sts in Gold, distribute evenly onto 4
   DPNs (16 sts per needle), and join into
   round.
For the cuff, work 5 rnds Gold, 5 rnds Off-
   White in Cuff Ribbing, then work 3 rnds
   alternating "k1 in Black, p1 in Off-White"
   (1.2 in. / 3 cm).

Begin the leg in colorwork pattern A in Black and Off-White. Work Rnds 1–11 of the chart once. Break the working yarn in Black, and work 2 rnds in stockinette stitch in Gold. Now, work 1 rnd alternating "k1 in Off-White, k1 in Black," then continue in colorwork pattern B in Off-White and Gold. Work Rnds 1–12 of the chart 3 times, then only Rnds 1–3 once more. Finish the leg in stockinette stitch with 1 rnd alternating "k1 in Off-White, k1 in Gold." Break working yarn in all colors.

Now, work a boomerang heel in stockinette stitch in Gold over the 32 sts of Ndls 4 and 1 according to instructions on page 183. Work the foot in stockinette stitch in the round over all sts of all 4 DPNs. Start with 1 rnd alternating "k1 in Off-White, k1 in Gold." After this, continue in stranded pattern B in Off-White and Gold. Work Rnds 7–12 of the chart once, Rnds 1–12 a total of 3 times, then only Rnds 1–3 once. Now, work 1 rnd alternating "k1 in Off-White, k1 in Gold." Break working yarn in Off-White and con-

tinue with Gold. After 6.9 in. / 17.5 cm from middle of heel, start toe decreases.

Work toe with paired banded decreases in Gold according to instructions on page 189. Break the working yarn, and pull the end through to the inside of the sock.

Weave in all ends.

Work the second sock the same way.

KNOCK YOUR SOCKS OFF IN WEARABLE RETRO

## WOMEN'S 5½/6
CO 64 sts (16 sts per needle).
Foot, Colorwork Chart B: Work Rnds 7–12 of the chart once, Rnds 1–12 twice, and Rnds 1–9 once. Continue in pattern, starting toe decreases 6.3 in. / 16 cm from middle of heel.

## WOMEN'S 9/9½, MEN'S 7/7½
CO 68 sts (17 sts per needle).
Foot, Colorwork Chart B: Work Rnds 7–12 of the chart once, Rnds 1–12 a total of 3 times, and Rnds 1–9 once. Continue in pattern, starting toe decreases 7.5 in. / 19 cm from middle of heel.

## WOMEN'S 11/12, MEN'S 8½/9
CO 68 sts (17 sts per needle).
Foot, Colorwork Chart B: Work Rnds 7–12 of the chart once, Rnds 1–12 a total of 4 times, and Rnds 1–3 once. Continue in pattern, starting toe decreases 8.1 in. / 20.5 cm from middle of heel.

## MEN'S 10/11
CO 72 sts (18 sts per needle).
Foot, Colorwork Chart B: Work Rnds 7–12 of the chart once, Rnds 1–12 a total of 4 times, and Rnds 1–9 once. Continue in pattern, starting toe decreases 8.7 in. / 22 cm from middle of heel.

# SOXX NO. 9

## DIFFICULTY LEVEL 3

## SIZES

Women's 5½–Men's 11

Pattern instructions as given are for size Women's 7/8; changes to stitch counts and variations needed for the other sizes are given on page 63.

## YARN AND NEEDLES

Lang Yarns Jawoll; #1 fingering weight yarn; 75% wool, 25% nylon; 230 yd. / 210 m, 1.75 oz. / 50 g per skein; 1 skein each in #150 Gold, #372 Aqua, #288 Petrol, and #94 Off-White

DPN set of 5 needles in size US 1.5–2.5 / 2.5–3.0 mm

## GAUGE

In stranded pattern on US 1.5–2.5 / 2.5–3.0 mm needles 34 sts and 36 rnds = 4 × 4 in. / 10 × 10 cm

## Stockinette Stitch

In rows: Knit on RS, purl on WS.
In rnds: Knit all sts in all rnds.

## Cuff Ribbing

Alternate "k1-tbl, p1."

## Knitting through the Back Loop (tbl)

Insert the needle from right to left into the
back leg of the stitch; knit the stitch this way
so it ends up twisted.

## Colorwork Charts A, B, and C

Stitch count has to be a multiple of 4.
Work all rnds in St st from the appropriate
    colorwork chart. Repeat the pattern repeat
    (4 sts wide) around.

### Colorwork Chart A

4
3
2
1

pattern
repeat =
4 stitches

■ = Petrol
□ = Off–White

### Colorwork Chart B

4
3
2
1

pattern
repeat =
4 stitches

▨ = Aqua
□ = Off–White

### Colorwork Chart C

4
3
2
1

pattern
repeat =
4 stitches

▨ = Gold
□ = Off–White

KNOCK YOUR SOCKS OFF IN WEARABLE RETRO

# INSTRUCTIONS

CO 64 sts in Petrol, distribute evenly onto 4 DPNs (16 sts per needle), and join into round.

For the cuff, work 10 rnds (1 in. / 2.5 cm) in Cuff Ribbing pattern.

Begin the leg with 4 rnds in Petrol in stockinette stitch, then continue in Petrol and Off-White from Chart A. Work Rnds 1–4 of chart 6 times, then Rnds 1–2 once more. Break working yarn in Petrol, and continue in Aqua and Off-White from Chart B. Work Rnds 3–4 of the chart once, then work Rnds 1–4 a total of 4 times. Break working yarn in Off-White. Finish the leg with 5 rnds in Aqua in stockinette stitch.

Now, work a boomerang heel in Aqua in stockinette stitch over the 32 sts of Ndls 4 and 1, following instructions on page 183.

Work the foot in stockinette stitch in the round over all sts on all 4 DPNs. Begin with 5 rnds in Aqua, then continue in Aqua and Off-White from Chart B. Work Rnds 1–4 of chart 4 times, then Rnds 1–2 once. Break working yarn in Aqua. Now, continue in Gold and Off-White from Chart C. Work Rnds 3–4 of the chart once, then Rnds 1–4 a total of 6 times. Break working yarn in Off-White, and finish the sock in Gold. After 8 in. / 20 cm from middle of heel, start decreases for the rounded toe.

Work rounded toe according to instructions on page 189. Graft the remaining opening in Kitchener stitch (see page 190).
Weave in all ends.
Work the second sock the same way.

KNOCK YOUR SOCKS OFF IN WEARABLE RETRO

# STITCH COUNTS AND VARIATIONS FOR OTHER SIZES

## WOMEN'S 5½/6
CO 64 sts (16 sts per needle).
Foot: Work as written. In Gold and Off-White, and following Chart C, work Rnds 3-4 once, and Rnds 1-4 a total of 5 times. Finish the sock in Gold, starting decreases for the rounded toe after 7.3 in. / 18.5 cm from middle of heel.

## WOMEN'S 9/9½, MEN'S 7/7½
CO 68 sts (17 sts per needle).
Foot: Work as written. In Aqua and Off-White, and following Chart B, work Rnds 1-4 a total of 5 times, and Rnds 1-2 once. Work from Chart C as for regular size, and finish the sock in Gold, starting decreases for the rounded toe after 8.5 in. / 21.5 cm from middle of heel.

## WOMEN'S 11/12, MEN'S 8½/9
CO 68 sts (17 sts per needle).
Foot: Work as written. In Aqua and Off-White, and following Chart B, work Rnds 1-4 a total of 6 times, and Rnds 1-2 once. Work from Chart C as for regular size, and finish the sock in Gold, starting decreases for the rounded toe after 9.1 in. / 23 cm from middle of heel.

## MEN'S 10/11
CO 72 sts (18 sts per needle).
Foot: Work as written. In Aqua and Off-White, and following Chart B, work Rnds 1-4 a total of 6 times, and Rnds 1-2 once. In Gold and Off-White, and following Chart C, work Rnds 3-4 once, and Rnds 1-4 a total of 7 times. Finish the sock in Gold, starting decreases for the rounded toe after 9.5 in. / 24.1 cm from middle of heel.

# SOXX NO. 10

## DIFFICULTY LEVEL 1

### SIZES

Women's 5½–Men's 11

Pattern instructions as given are for size Women's 7/8; changes to stitch counts and variations needed for the other sizes are given on page 67.

### YARN AND NEEDLES

Lang Yarns Jawoll; #1 fingering weight yarn; 75% wool, 25% nylon; 230 yd. / 210 m, 1.75 oz. / 50 g per skein; 1 skein each in #150 Gold, #94 Off-White, and #288 Petrol

DPN set of 5 needles in size US 1.5–2.5 / 2.5–3.0 mm

### GAUGE

In stockinette stitch on US 1.5–2.5 / 2.5–3.0 mm needles 32 sts and 36 rnds = 4 × 4 in. / 10 × 10 cm

KNOCK YOUR SOCKS OFF IN WEARABLE RETRO

## Stockinette Stitch
In rows: Knit on RS, purl on WS.
In rnds: Knit all sts in all rnds.

## Cuff Ribbing
Alternate "k1, p1."

# INSTRUCTIONS

CO 60 sts in Gold, distribute evenly onto 4 DPNs (15 sts per needle), and join into round.

For the cuff, work 12 rnds (1.2 in. / 3 cm) in Cuff Ribbing pattern. Break the working yarn.

Work the leg in stockinette stitch. Work *5 rnds Off-White, 5 rnds Petrol, rep from * 6 times. Break working yarn in both colors, then work another 2 rnds in Gold.

Now, work a boomerang heel in stockinette stitch in Gold over the 30 sts of Ndls 4 and 1, following instructions on page 183.

Work the foot in stockinette stitch in the round over all sts on all 4 DPNs, beginning with 1 rnd in Gold. Break the working yarn. Now, work *5 rnds Petrol, 5 rnds Off-White, rep from * 4 times, then work another 5 rnds in Petrol. After this, break both yarns, and continue in Gold. After 8 in. / 20 cm from middle of heel, start decreases for the rounded toe.

Work rounded toe according to instructions on page 189. Graft the remaining opening in Kitchener stitch (see page 190).

Weave in all ends.

Work the second sock the same way.

**WOMEN'S 5½/6**
CO 60 sts (15 sts per needle).
Foot: *5 rnds Petrol, 5 rnds Off-White, rep from * 3 times.
Continue as written, starting decreases for the rounded toe
after 7.3 in. / 18.5 cm from middle of heel.

**WOMEN'S 9/9½, MEN'S 7/7½**
CO 64 sts (16 sts per needle).
Foot: *5 rnds Petrol, 5 rnds Off-White, rep from * 4 times.
Continue as written, starting decreases for the rounded toe
after 8.5 in. / 21.5 cm from middle of heel.

**WOMEN'S 11/12, MEN'S 8½/9**
CO 64 sts (16 sts per needle).
Foot: *5 rnds Petrol, 5 rnds Off-White, rep from * 5 times.
Continue as written, starting decreases for the rounded toe
after 9.1 in. / 23 cm from middle of heel.

**MEN'S 10/11**
CO 68 sts (17 sts per needle).
Foot: *5 rnds Petrol, 5 rnds Off-White, rep from * 5 times.
Continue as written, starting decreases for the rounded toe
after 9.6 in. / 24.5 cm from middle of heel.

# SOXX No. 11

## DIFFICULTY LEVEL 3

## SIZES

Women's 5½–Men's 11

Pattern instructions as given are for size Women's 7/8; changes to stitch counts and variations needed for the other sizes are given on page 73.

## YARN AND NEEDLES

Lang Yarns Jawoll; #1 fingering weight yarn; 75% wool, 25% nylon; 230 yd. / 210 m, 1.75 oz. / 50 g per skein; 1 skein each in #226 Beige, #150 Gold, #288 Petrol, and #388 Light Petrol

DPN set of 5 needles in size US 1.5–2.5 / 2.5–3.0 mm

## GAUGE

In stranded pattern on US 1.5–2.5 / 2.5–3.0 mm needles 34 stitches and 38 rnds = 4 × 4 in. / 10 × 10 cm

## Stockinette Stitch

In rows: Knit on RS, purl on WS.
In rnds: Knit all sts in all rnds.

## Cuff Ribbing

Alternate "k1, p1."

## Colorwork Charts A, B, and C

Stitch count has to be a multiple of 4.
Work all rnds in St st from the appropriate
    colorwork chart. Repeat the pattern repeat
    (4 sts wide) around.

### Colorwork Chart A

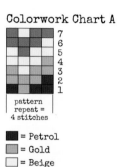

```
7
6
5
4
3
2
1
```

pattern
repeat =
4 stitches

■ = Petrol
■ = Gold
□ = Beige
■ = Light Petrol

### Colorwork Chart B

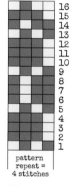

```
16
15
14
13
12
11
10
9
8
7
6
5
4
3
2
1
```

pattern
repeat =
4 stitches

■ = Light Petrol
□ = Beige

### Colorwork Chart C

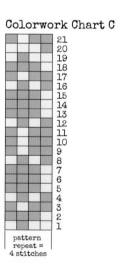

```
21
20
19
18
17
16
15
14
13
12
11
10
9
8
7
6
5
4
3
2
1
```

pattern
repeat =
4 stitches

□ = Beige
■ = Gold

KNOCK YOUR SOCKS OFF IN WEARABLE RETRO

# INSTRUCTIONS

CO 64 sts in Petrol, distribute evenly onto 4 DPNs (16 sts per needle), and join into round.

For the cuff, work 15 rnds (1.2 in. / 3 cm) in Cuff Ribbing pattern.

Begin the leg with 3 rnds in Petrol in stockinette stitch, then continue in Petrol, Gold, Beige, and Light Petrol from Chart A. Work Rnds 1–7 of the chart once. Break working yarn in Petrol and Gold. Now, continue in Light Petrol and Beige from Chart B. Work Rnds 1–8 of the chart 3 times, then Rnds 9–16 once. Now, work 1 rnd Beige, *3 rnds Gold, 1 rnd Beige, rep from * once. Break working yarn in both colors.

Now, work a boomerang heel in Petrol in stockinette stitch over the 32 sts of Ndls 4 and 1, following instructions on page 183.

Work the foot in stockinette stitch in the round over all sts on all 4 DPNs. First, work 1 rnd in Petrol, then break the working yarn. Now, work *1 rnd Beige, 3 rnds Light Petrol, rep from * once, then work 1 rnd in Beige. Continue in Beige and Gold from

Chart C. Work Rnds 1–4 of chart once, then Rnds 5–12 three times, and Rnds 13–21 once. Now, continue in stockinette stitch as follows: 4 rnds in Gold, *1 rnd Petrol, 1 rnd Gold, rep from * twice. Break the working yarn in Gold, and finish the sock in Petrol. After 6.9 in. / 17.5 cm from middle of heel, start toe decreases.

Work toe with paired banded decreases in Petrol according to instructions on page 189. Break the working yarn, and pull the end through to the inside of the sock.
Weave in all ends.
Work the second sock the same way.

KNOCK YOUR SOCKS OFF IN WEARABLE RETRO

## WOMEN'S 5½/6

CO 64 sts (16 sts per needle).

Foot, Colorwork Chart C: Work Rnds 1-4 of chart once, then Rnds 5-12 twice, and after this, Rnds 13-19 once. Continue as stated in pattern, starting toe decreases 6.3 in. / 16 cm from middle of heel.

## WOMEN'S 9/9½, MEN'S 7/7½

CO 68 sts (17 sts per needle).

Foot, Colorwork Chart C: Work Rnds 1-4 of chart once, then Rnds 5-12 a total of 3 times, and Rnds 13-19 once. Continue as stated in pattern, starting toe decreases 7.5 in. / 19 cm from middle of heel.

## WOMEN'S 11/12, MEN'S 8½/9

CO 68 sts (17 sts per needle).

Foot, Colorwork Chart C: Work Rnds 1-4 of chart once, then Rnds 5-12 a total 4 times, and Rnds 13-19 once. Continue as stated in pattern, starting toe decreases 8.1 in. / 20.5 cm from middle of heel.

## MEN'S 10/11

CO 72 sts (18 sts per needle).

Foot, Colorwork Chart C: Work Rnds 1-4 of chart once, then Rnds 5-12 a total 4 times, and Rnds 13-19 once. Continue as stated in pattern, starting toe decreases 8.7 in. / 22 cm from middle of heel.

NATURGEWA

Nature at

*your feet* »»»»»»»

# SOXX NO.12

## DIFFICULTY LEVEL 2

## SIZES

Women's 9/9½–Men's 12/13

Pattern instructions as given are for size Women's 11/12, Men's 8½/9; changes to stitch counts and variations needed for the other sizes are given on page 80.

## YARN AND NEEDLES

Lang Yarns Jawoll; #1 fingering weight yarn; 75% wool, 25% nylon; 230 yd. / 210 m, 1.75 oz. / 50 g per skein; 1 skein each in #45 Light Brown Heathered and #94 Off-White, and 2 skeins #07 Steel Blue

DPN set of 5 needles in size US 1.5–2.5 / 2.5–3.0 mm

## GAUGE

In stranded pattern on US 1.5–2.5 / 2.5–3.0 mm needles
32 sts and 42 rnds = 4 × 4 in. / 10 × 10 cm

## Colorwork Chart

Stitch count has to be a multiple of 4.

Work all rnds in St st from colorwork chart. Repeat the pattern repeat (4 sts wide) around.

### Colorwork Chart

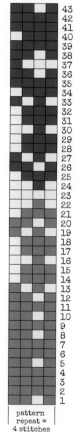

43
42
41
40
39
38
37
36
35
34
33
32
31
30
29
28
27
26
25
24
23
22
21
20
19
18
17
16
15
14
13
12
11
10
9
8
7
6
5
4
3
2
1

pattern
repeat =
4 stitches

■ = Light Brown Heathered
□ = Off-White
■ = Steel Blue

## Stockinette Stitch

In rows: Knit on RS, purl on WS.
In rnds: Knit all sts in all rnds.

## Knitting through the Back Loop (tbl)

Insert the needle from right to left into the back leg of the stitch; knit the stitch this way so it ends up twisted.

## Cuff Ribbing

Alternate "k1-tbl, p1."

# INSTRUCTIONS

CO 68 sts in Light Brown Heathered, distribute evenly onto 4 DPNs (17 sts per needle) and join into round.

For the cuff, work 15 rnds (1.4 in. / 3.5 cm) in Cuff Ribbing pattern.

Begin the leg with 20 rnds in stockinette stitch, then work stranded pattern in Light Brown Heathered, Off-White, and Steel Blue. Work Rnds 1–43 of the chart once.

Break working yarn in both Light Brown Heathered and Off-White. Continue the leg in Steel Blue. After having reached an overall length of 8.1 in. / 20.5 cm, start the boomerang heel.

Work boomerang heel in Steel Blue in stockinette stitch over the 34 sts of Ndls 4 and 1, following instructions on page 183.

## STITCH COUNTS AND VARIATIONS FOR OTHER SIZES

**WOMEN'S 9/9½, MEN'S 7/7½**
CO 68 sts (17 sts per needle).
Foot: After 7.5 in. / 19 cm from middle of heel, start toe decreases.

**MEN'S 10/11**
CO 72 sts (18 sts per needle).
Foot: After 8.7 in. / 22 cm from middle of heel, start toe decreases.

**MEN'S 12/13**
CO 76 sts (19 sts per needle).
Foot: After 9.3 in. / 23.5 cm from middle of heel, start toe decreases.

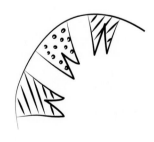

Continue the foot in Steel Blue in stockinette stitch in the round over all sts on all 4 DPNs. After 8.1 in. / 20.5 cm from middle of heel, start toe decreases.

Work paired banded toe decreases according to instructions on page 189. Break the working yarn, and pull the end through to the inside of the sock.

Weave in all ends.

Work the second sock the same way.

# SOXX NO.13

## DIFFICULTY LEVEL 2

## SIZES

Women's 5½–Men's 11

Pattern instructions as given are for size Women's 7/8; changes to stitch counts and variations needed for the other sizes are given on page 85.

## YARN AND NEEDLES

Lang Yarns Jawoll; #1 fingering weight yarn; 75% wool, 25% nylon; 230 yd. / 210 m, 1.75 oz. / 50 g per skein; 1 skein each in #61 Burgundy and #22 Light Beige Heathered (For sizes Women's 9/9½, Men's 7/7½ and up, you will need 2 skeins of Light Beige Heathered.)

DPN set of 5 needles in size US 1.5–2.5 / 2.5–3.0 mm

## GAUGE

In stranded pattern on US 1.5–2.5 / 2.5–3.0 mm needles 32 sts and 36 rnds = 4 × 4 in. / 10 × 10 cm

## Stockinette Stitch

In rows: Knit on RS, purl on WS.
In rnds: Knit all sts in all rnds.

## Cuff Ribbing

Alternate "k2, p2."

## Colorwork Charts A and B

Stitch count has to be a multiple of 4.
Work all rnds in St st from the appropriate
colorwork chart. Repeat the pattern repeat
(4 sts wide) around.

Colorwork Chart A

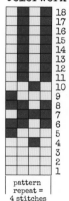

18
17
16
15
14
13
12
11
10
9
8
7
6
5
4
3
2
1

pattern
repeat =
4 stitches

☐ = Light Beige Heathered
■ = Burgundy

Colorwork Chart B

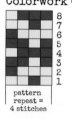

8
7
6
5
4
3
2
1

pattern
repeat =
4 stitches

☐ = Light Beige
  Heathered
■ = Burgundy

# INSTRUCTIONS

CO 74 sts in Burgundy, distribute evenly onto
4 DPNs (16 sts per needle), and join into
round.

For the cuff, work 15 rnds (1.4 in. / 3.5 cm) in
Cuff Ribbing pattern.

For the leg, first knit 1 rnd in Burgundy, then
work 8 rnds in stockinette stitch, alternating 1 st in Light Beige Heathered and 1 st
in Burgundy. After this, continue in stranded pattern from Chart A. Work Rnds 1–18
of the chart twice. Break working yarn in
both colors.

Work turned heel with heel flap in stockinette
stitch in Burgundy over the 32 sts of Ndls 4
and 1 according to instructions on page
186. Break the working yarn in Burgundy.

Work the foot in stockinette stitch in the
round in Light Beige Heathered over all sts
on all 4 DPNs. After 6.5 in. / 16.5 cm from
middle of heel, continue in Burgundy and
Light Beige Heathered from Chart B. Work
Rnds 1–8 of the chart once. Break the
working yarn in Light Beige Heathered,
and finish the sock in Burgundy. After 8 in.
/ 20 cm from middle of heel, start decreases for the rounded toe.

Work rounded toe according to instructions
on page 189. Graft the remaining opening
in Kitchener stitch (see page 190).

Weave in all ends.

Work the second sock the same way.

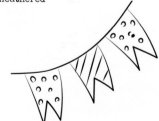

### WOMEN'S 5½/6
CO 64 sts (16 sts per needle).
Foot: After 5.9 in. / 15 cm from middle of heel, work in Burgundy and Light Beige Heathered from Chart B. Work Rnds 1-8 once. Continue as stated in pattern, starting decreases for the rounded toe after 7.3 in. / 18.5 cm from middle of heel.

### WOMEN'S 9/9½, MEN'S 7/7½
CO 68 sts (17 sts per needle).
Foot: After 7.1 in. / 18 cm from middle of heel, work in Burgundy and Light Beige Heathered from Chart B. Work Rnds 1-8 once. Continue as stated in pattern, starting decreases for the rounded toe after 8.5 in. / 21.5 cm from middle of heel.

### WOMEN'S 11/12, MEN'S 8½/9
CO 68 sts (17 sts per needle).
Foot: After 7.7 in. / 19.5 cm from middle of heel, work in Burgundy and Light Beige Heathered from Chart B. Work Rnds 1-8 once. Continue as stated in pattern, starting decreases for the rounded toe after 9.1 in. / 23 cm from middle of heel.

### MEN'S 10/11
CO 72 sts (18 sts per needle).
Foot: After 8.3 in. / 21 cm from middle of heel, work in Burgundy and Light Beige Heathered from Chart B. Work Rnds 1-8 once. Continue as stated in pattern, starting decreases for the rounded toe after 9.6 in. / 24.5 cm from middle of heel.

# SOXX no.14

## DIFFICULTY LEVEL 2

## SIZES

Women's 5½–Men's 11

Pattern instructions as given are for size Women's 7/8; changes to stitch counts and variations needed for the other sizes are given on page 89.

## YARN AND NEEDLES

Schachenmayr Regia 4-ply; #1 fingering weight yarn; 75% wool, 25% polyamide; 230 yd. / 210 m, 1.75 oz. / 50 g per skein; 1 skein each in #2070 Wood Streaked, #324 Marine Blue, and #2080 Super White

DPN set of 5 needles in size US 1.5–2.5 / 2.5–3.0 mm

## GAUGE

In stranded pattern on US 1.5–2.5 / 2.5–3.0 mm needles 32 sts and 38 rnds = 4 × 4 in. / 10 × 10 cm

## Stockinette Stitch
In rows: Knit on RS, purl on WS.
In rnds: Knit all sts in all rnds.

## Cuff Ribbing
Alternate "k1, p1."

## Colorwork Chart
Stitch count has to be a multiple of 4.
Work all rnds in St st from colorwork chart.
Repeat the pattern repeat (4 sts wide) around.

Colorwork Chart

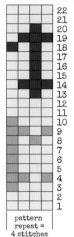

22
21
20
19
18
17
16
15
14
13
12
11
10
9
8
7
6
5
4
3
2
1

pattern
repeat =
4 stitches

☐ = Super White
▨ = Wood Streaked
■ = Marine Blue

# INSTRUCTIONS
CO 60 sts in Wood Streaked, distribute evenly onto 4 DPNs (15 sts per needle), and join into round.

For the cuff, work 13 rnds (1.2 in. / 3 cm) in Cuff Ribbing pattern.

Work the leg in stockinette stitch in the round: *1 rnd Wood Streaked, 3 rnds Marine Blue, rep from * 3 times. Continue in stranded pattern in Super White, Wood Streaked, and Marine Blue. Work Rnds 1–22 of the chart once. Break the working yarn in Super White.

Now, work *3 rnds Marine Blue, 1 rnd Wood Streaked, rep from * twice. Finish the leg with 3 rnds Marine Blue. Break working yarn in all colors.

Now, work turned heel with heel flap in stockinette stitch in Wood Streaked over the 30 sts of Ndls 4 and 1 according to instructions on page 186.

Work the foot in stockinette stitch in the round over all sts of all 4 DPNs. Work *3 rnds in Wood Streaked, 1 rnd in Marine Blue, rep from * 12 times. Break the working yarn in Marine Blue, and finish the sock in Wood Streaked. After 6.9 in. / 17.5 cm from middle of heel, start toe decreases.

Work paired banded toe decreases according to instructions on page 189. Break the working yarn, and pull the end through to the inside of the sock.

Weave in all ends.

Work the second sock the same way.

# STITCH COUNTS AND VARIATIONS FOR OTHER SIZES

## WOMEN'S 5½/6
CO 60 sts (15 sts per needle).
Foot: *3 rnds in Wood Streaked, 1 rnd in Marine Blue, rep from * 10 times. Continue as stated in pattern, starting toe decreases 6.3 in. / 16 cm from middle of heel.

## WOMEN'S 9/9½, MEN'S 7/7½
CO 64 sts (16 sts per needle).
Foot: *3 rnds in Wood Streaked, 1 rnd in Marine Blue, rep from * 13 times. Continue as stated in pattern, starting toe decreases 7.5 in. / 19 cm from middle of heel.

## WOMEN'S 11/12, MEN'S 8½/9
CO 64 sts (16 sts per needle).
Foot: *3 rnds in Wood Streaked, 1 rnd in Marine Blue, rep from * 15 times. Continue as stated in pattern, starting toe decreases 8.1 in. / 20.5 cm from middle of heel.

## MEN'S 10/11
CO 68 sts (17 sts per needle).
Foot: *3 rnds in Wood Streaked, 1 rnd in Marine Blue, rep from * 16 times. Continue as stated in pattern, starting toe decreases 8.7 in. / 22 cm from middle of heel.

# SOXX NO. 15

## DIFFICULTY LEVEL 3

## SIZES

Women's 5½–Men's 11

Pattern instructions as given are for size Women's 7/8; changes to stitch counts and variations needed for the other sizes are given on page 95.

## YARN AND NEEDLES

Lang Yarns Jawoll; #1 fingering weight yarn; 75% wool, 25% nylon; 230 yd. / 210 m, 1.75 oz. / 50 g per skein; 1 skein each in #25 Navy, #01 White, #32 Jeans, and #22 Light Beige Heathered

DPN set of 5 needles in size US 1.5–2.5 / 2.5–3.0 mm

## GAUGE

In stranded pattern on US 1.5–2.5 / 2.5–3.0 mm needles 32 sts and 38 rnds = 4 × 4 in. / 10 × 10 cm

## Stockinette Stitch

In rows: Knit on RS, purl on WS.
In rnds: Knit all sts in all rnds.

## Cuff Ribbing

Alternate "k2, p2."

## Colorwork Charts A and B

Stitch count has to be a multiple of 4.

In all rnds, work in stockinette stitch from appropriate colorwork chart. Repeat the pattern repeat (4 sts wide) around.

### Colorwork Chart A

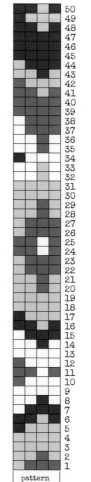

pattern
repeat =
4 stitches

■ = Jeans
□ = Light Beige Heathered
■ = Navy
□ = White

### Colorwork Chart B

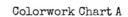

pattern
repeat =
4 stitches

■ = Navy
□ = Light Beige Heathered
■ = Jeans

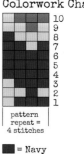

NATURE AT YOUR FEET

# INSTRUCTIONS

CO 64 sts in Jeans, distribute evenly onto 4 DPNs (16 sts per needle), and join into round.

For the cuff, work 15 rnds (1.4 in. / 3.5 cm) in Cuff Ribbing pattern.

Begin the leg in stockinette stitch with 2 rnds Jeans, then continue in stranded pattern from Chart A in colors Jeans, Light Beige Heathered, Navy, and White. Work Rnds 1–50 of the chart once. Break working yarn in colors Jeans, White, and Light Beige Heathered, and proceed, working 10 rnds in Navy.

Work turned heel with heel flap in stockinette stitch in Navy over the 32 sts of Ndls 4 and 1 according to instructions on page 186.

Continue the foot in Navy in stockinette stitch in the round over all sts on all 4 DPNs. After 5.5 in. / 14 cm from middle of heel, continue in Navy, Light Beige Heathered, and Jeans from Chart B. Work Rnds 1–10 of the chart once. Break working yarn in Navy and Light Beige Heathered. Now, continue in Jeans, starting decreases for the rounded toe after 8 in. / 20 cm from middle of heel.

Work rounded toe according to instructions on page 189. Graft the remaining opening in Kitchener stitch on page 190.
Weave in all ends.
Work the second sock the same way.

# STITCH COUNTS AND VARIATIONS FOR OTHER SIZES

### WOMEN'S 5½/6
CO 64 sts (16 sts per needle).
Foot: After 5 in. / 12.5 cm from middle of heel, continue from Chart B in Navy, Light Beige Heathered, and Jeans. Work Rnds 1–10 once. Continue as stated in pattern, starting decreases for the rounded toe after 7.3 in. / 18.5 cm from middle of heel.

### WOMEN'S 9/9½, MEN'S 7/7½
CO 68 sts (17 sts per needle).
Foot: After 6.1 in. / 15.5 cm from middle of heel, continue from Chart B in Navy, Light Beige Heathered, and Jeans. Work Rnds 1–10 once. Continue as stated in pattern, starting decreases for the rounded toe after 8.5 in. / 21.5 cm from middle of heel.

### WOMEN'S 11/12, MEN'S 8½/9
CO 68 sts (17 sts per needle).
Foot: After 6.7 in. / 17 cm from middle of heel, continue from Chart B in Navy, Light Beige Heathered, and Jeans. Work Rnds 1–10 once. Continue as stated in pattern, starting decreases for the rounded toe after 9.1 in. / 23 cm from middle of heel.

### MEN'S 10/11
CO 72 sts (18 sts per needle).
Foot: After 7.3 in. / 18.5 cm from middle of heel, continue from Chart B in Navy, Light Beige Heathered, and Jeans. Work Rnds 1–10 once. Continue as stated in pattern, starting decreases for the rounded toe after 9.6 in. / 24.5 cm from middle of heel.

Anchors aweigh!

# SOXX NO.16

## DIFFICULTY LEVEL 3

## SIZES

Women's 5½–Men's 11

Pattern instructions as given are for size Women's 7/8; changes to stitch counts and variations needed for the other sizes are given on page 103.

## YARN AND NEEDLES

Lang Yarns Jawoll; #1 fingering weight yarn; 75% wool, 25% nylon; 230 yd. / 210 m, 1.75 oz. / 50 g per skein; 1 skein each in #110 Blue, #60 Red, and #01 White

DPN set of 5 needles in size US 1.5–2.5 / 2.5–3.0 mm

## GAUGE

In stranded pattern on US 1.5–2.5 / 2.5–3.0 mm needles
34 sts and 38 rnds = 4 × 4 in. / 10 × 10 cm

## Colorwork Charts A and B

Stitch count has to be a multiple of 4.

Work all rnds in St st from the appropriate colorwork chart. Repeat the pattern repeat (4 sts wide) around.

### Colorwork Chart A

```
4
3
2
1
pattern
repeat =
4 stitches
```

■ = Blue
□ = White
■ = Red

### Colorwork Chart B

```
8
7
6
5
4
3
2
1
pattern
repeat =
4 stitches
```

■ = Blue
□ = White
■ = Red

## Colorwork Chart C

Stitch count has to be a multiple of 2.

Work all rnds in St st from colorwork chart. Repeat the pattern repeat (2 sts wide) around.

If the stitch count per needle is odd, start with the second stitch.

### Colorwork Chart C

```
4
3
2
1
pattern
repeat =
2 stitches
```

□ = White
■ = Red
■ = Blue

## Stockinette Stitch

In rows: Knit on RS, purl on WS.
In rnds: Knit all sts in all rnds.

## Cuff Ribbing

Alternate "k1, p1."

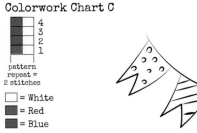

# INSTRUCTIONS

CO 64 sts in Red, distribute evenly onto 4
DPNs (16 sts per needle), and join into
round.

For the cuff, work 10 rnds (0.8 in. / 2 cm) in
Cuff Ribbing pattern.

Begin the leg in stockinette stitch with 5 rnds
of alternating 1 st White, 1 st Blue, then
continue in stranded pattern from Chart A
in Blue, White, and Red. Work Rnds 1–4 of
chart 3 times. After this, continue from
Chart B. Work Rnds 1–8 of the chart 4
times, then work only Rnds 1–7 once.
Break working yarn in all colors.

Work turned heel with heel flap in stockinette
stitch in Blue over the 32 sts of Ndls 4 and
1 according to instructions on page 186.
Pick up and knit sts from the edges of the
heel flap according to Chart C, alternating
1 st Red, 1 st White.

Work the foot in stockinette stitch in the
round over all sts on all 4 DPNs. Continue
over the instep sts (Ndls 2 and 3) in stranded pattern from Chart B in Blue, White, and
Red. Work Rnd 8 of the chart once, Rnds
1–8 a total of 6 times, and finally, Rnds 1–3
once. At the same time, work the sole

(Ndls 4 and 1) in stranded pattern from Chart C. Work Rnds 1–4 of the chart 13 times. For a neat transition between sole and instep, work the last st of Ndl 1 and the first st of Ndl 4 according to Chart B. Break the working yarn in Blue and continue, alternating 1 rnd White, 1 rnd Red. After 6.9 in. / 17.5 cm from middle of heel, start toe decreases.

Work toe with paired banded decreases according to instructions on page 189, at the same time continuing the stripe pattern in White and Red. Break the working yarn in White and Red, and pull the end through to the inside of the sock.

Weave in all ends.

Work the second sock the same way.

ANCHORS AWEIGH!

# STITCH COUNTS AND VARIATIONS FOR OTHER SIZES

**WOMEN'S 5½/6**
CO 64 sts (16 sts per needle).
Foot, Colorwork Chart B: Work Rnd 8 once, Rnds 1–8 a total of 5 times, then only Rnds 1–3 once. Continue as stated in pattern, starting toe decreases 6.3 in. / 16 cm from middle of heel.

**WOMEN'S 9/9½, MEN'S 7/7½**
CO 68 sts (17 sts per needle).
Foot, Colorwork Chart B: Work Rnd 8 once, Rnds 1–8 a total of 6 times, then only Rnds 1–7 once. Continue as stated in pattern, starting toe decreases 7.5 in. / 19 cm from middle of heel.

**WOMEN'S 11/12, MEN'S 8½/9**
CO 68 sts (17 sts per needle).
Foot, Colorwork Chart B: Work Rnd 8 once, Rnds 1–8 a total of 7 times, then only Rnds 1–3 once. Continue as stated in pattern, starting toe decreases 8.1 in. / 20.5 cm from middle of heel.

**MEN'S 10/11**
CO 72 sts (18 sts per needle).
Foot, Colorwork Chart B: Work Rnd 8 once, Rnds 1–8 a total of 8 times, then only Rnds 1–3 once. Continue as stated in pattern, starting toe decreases 8.7 in. / 22 cm from middle of heel.

# SOXX no. 17

## DIFFICULTY LEVEL 2

## SIZES

Women's 5½–Men's 11

Pattern instructions as given are for size Women's 7/8; changes to stitch counts and variations needed for the other sizes are given on page 106.

## YARN AND NEEDLES

Schachenmayr Regia 4-ply; #1 fingering weight yarn; 75% wool, 25% polyamide; 230 yd. / 210 m, 1.75 oz. / 50 g per skein; 1 skein each in #2002 Cherry, #2080 Super White, and #324 Marine Blue

DPN set of 5 needles in size US 1.5–2.5 / 2.5–3.0 mm

## GAUGE

In stranded pattern on US 1.5–2.5 / 2.5–3.0 mm needles
32 sts and 34 rnds = 4 × 4 in. / 10 × 10 cm

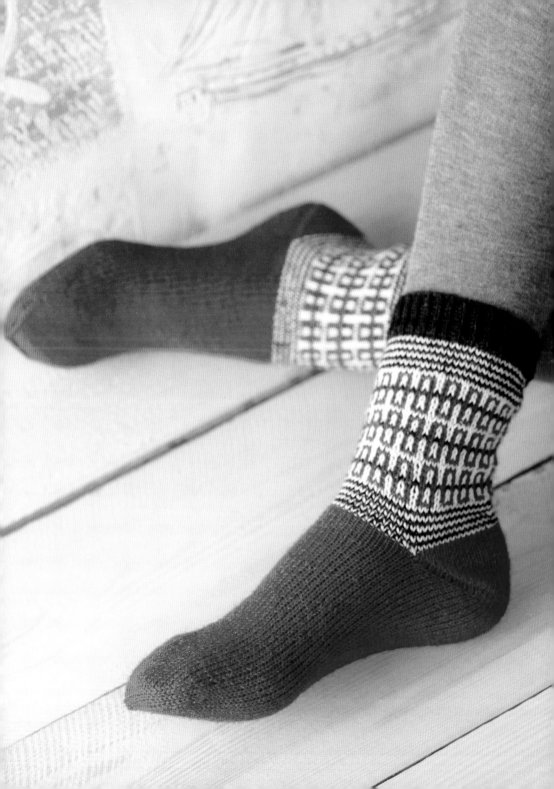

## STITCH COUNTS AND VARIATIONS FOR OTHER SIZES

### WOMEN'S 5½/6
CO 60 sts (15 sts per needle).
Foot: After 6.3 in. / 16 cm from middle of heel, start toe decreases.

### WOMEN'S 9/9½, MEN'S 7/7½
CO 64 sts (16 sts per needle).
Foot: After 7.5 in. / 19 cm from middle of heel, start toe decreases.

### WOMEN'S 11/12, MEN'S 8½/9
CO 64 sts (16 sts per needle).
Foot: After 8.1 in. / 20.5 cm from middle of heel, start toe decreases.

### MEN'S 10/11
CO 68 sts (17 sts per needle).
Foot: After 8.7 in. / 22 cm from middle of heel, start toe decreases.

## Stockinette Stitch

In rows: Knit on RS, purl on WS.
In rnds: Knit all sts in all rnds.

## Cuff Ribbing

Alternate "k1-tbl, p1."

## Knitting through the Back Loop (tbl)

Insert the needle from right to left into the back leg of the stitch; knit the stitch this way so it ends up twisted.

## Colorwork Chart

Stitch count has to be a multiple of 4.
Work all rnds in St st from the appropriate colorwork chart. Repeat the pattern repeat (4 sts wide) around.

### Colorwork Chart

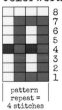

pattern
repeat =
4 stitches

■ = Cherry
□ = Super White
■ = Marine Blue

# INSTRUCTIONS

CO 60 sts in Marine Blue, distribute evenly onto 4 DPNs (15 sts per needle), and join into round.

For the cuff, work 10 rnds (1 in. / 2.5 cm) in Cuff Ribbing pattern.

Work the leg in stockinette stitch as *1 rnd Marine Blue, 1 rnd Super White, rep from * 3 times. Now, continue in stranded pattern in Cherry, Super White, and Marine Blue. Work Rnds 1–8 of the chart 3 times. After this, work *1 rnd Marine Blue, 1 rnd Super White, rep from * 3 times. Break working yarn in Marine Blue and Super White.

Work a boomerang heel in stockinette stitch in Cherry over the 30 sts of Ndls 4 and 1 according to instructions on page 183.

Now, work the foot in stockinette stitch in the round in Cherry over all sts on all 4 DPNs. After 6.9 in. / 17.5 cm from middle of heel, start toe decreases.

Work toe with paired banded decreases according to instructions on page 189. Break the working yarn, and pull the end through to the inside of the sock.

Weave in all ends.

Work the second sock the same way.

# SOXX NO. 18

## DIFFICULTY LEVEL 1

## SIZES

Women's 5½–Men's 11

Pattern instructions as given are for size Women's 7/8; changes to stitch counts and variations needed for the other sizes are given on page 111.

## YARN AND NEEDLES

Schachenmayr Regia 4-ply; #1 fingering weight yarn; 75% wool, 25% polyamide; 230 yd. / 210 m, 1.75 oz. / 50 g per skein; 1 skein each in #2002 Cherry, #2080 Super White, and #1945 Light Blue

DPN set of 5 needles in size US 1.5–2.5 / 2.5–3.0 mm

## GAUGE

In stockinette stitch on US 1.5–2.5 / 2.5–3.0 mm needles 30 sts and 34 rnds = 4 × 4 in. / 10 × 10 cm

ANCHORS AWEIGH!

# INSTRUCTIONS

CO 60 sts in Light Blue, distribute evenly onto 4 DPNs (15 sts per needle), and join into round.

Work the Cuff in Cuff Ribbing pattern in the following stripe sequence: 1 rnd Light Blue, 9 rnds Super White, 3 rnds Light Blue (1.2 in. / 3 cm).

Now, continue the leg in stockinette stitch as follows: *3 rnds Super White, 3 rnds Light Blue, rep from * once. Break working yarn in Light Blue and work *3 rnds Super White, 3 rnds Cherry, rep from * 8 times. Break working yarn in Cherry and Super White.

Work turned heel with heel flap in stockinette stitch in Light Blue over the 30 sts of Ndls 4 and 1 according to instructions on page 186. Break working yarn in Light Blue.

Work the foot in stockinette stitch in the round over all sts on all 4 DPNs, continuing the stripe pattern, alternating 3 rnds Super White, 3 rnds Cherry, to the end. After 8 in. / 20 cm from middle of heel, start decreases for the rounded toe.

Work rounded toe according to instructions on page 189. Graft the remaining opening in Kitchener stitch (see page 190).

Weave in all ends.

Work the second sock the same way.

## Stockinette Stitch
In rows: Knit on RS, purl on WS.
In rnds: Knit all sts in all rnds.

## Cuff Ribbing
Alternate "k1, p1."

# STITCH COUNTS AND VARIATIONS FOR OTHER SIZES

### WOMEN'S 5½/6
CO 60 sts (15 sts per needle).
Foot: After 7.3 in. / 18.5 cm from middle of heel, start decreases for the rounded toe.

### WOMEN'S 9/9½, MEN'S 7/7½
CO 64 sts (16 sts per needle).
Foot: After 8.5 in. / 21.5 cm from middle of heel, start decreases for the rounded toe.

### WOMEN'S 11/12, MEN'S 8½/9
CO 64 sts (16 sts per needle).
Foot: After 9 in. / 23 cm from middle of heel, start decreases for the rounded toe.

### MEN'S 10/11
CO 68 sts (17 sts per needle).
Foot: After 9.7 in. / 24.5 cm from middle of heel, start decreases for the rounded toe.

# SOXX No.19

## DIFFICULTY LEVEL 2

## SIZES

Women's 5½–Men's 11

Pattern instructions as given are for size Women's 7/8; changes to stitch counts and variations needed for the other sizes are given on page 117.

## YARN AND NEEDLES

Schachenmayr Regia 4-ply; #1 fingering weight yarn; 75% wool, 25% polyamide; 230 yd. / 210 m, 1.75 oz. / 50 g per skein; 1 skein each in #2002 Cherry, #2080 Super White, and #1945 Light Blue

DPN set of 5 needles in size US 1.5–2.5 / 2.5–3.0 mm

## GAUGE

In stranded pattern on US 1.5–2.5 / 2.5–3.0 mm needles 32 sts and 34 rnds = 4 × 4 in. / 10 × 10 cm

ANCHORS AWEIGH!

## Stockinette Stitch

In rows: Knit on RS, purl on WS.
In rnds: Knit all sts in all rnds.

## Cuff Ribbing

Alternate "k1, p1."

## Colorwork Charts A and B

Stitch count has to be a multiple of 4.
Work all rnds in St st from the appropriate
colorwork chart. Repeat the pattern repeat
(4 sts wide) around.

### Colorwork Chart A

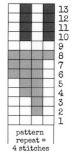

13
12
11
10
9
8
7
6
5
4
3
2
1

pattern
repeat =
4 stitches

☐ = Super White
▨ = Light Blue
■ = Cherry

### Colorwork Chart B

4
3
2
1

pattern
repeat =
4 stitches

☐ = Super White
▨ = Light Blue

# INSTRUCTIONS

CO 64 sts in Cherry, distribute evenly onto 4 DPNs (16 sts per needle), and join into round.

For the cuff, work in Cuff Ribbing, beginning with 11 rnds in Cherry, followed by 4 rnds (1.4 in. / 3.5 cm) alternating k1 in Cherry, p1 in Super White.

Work the leg in stockinette stitch in stranded pattern from Chart A in Super White, Light Blue, and Cherry. Work Rnds 1–13 of the chart 3 times, then work only Rnds 1–8 once more. Now, work *2 rnds Super White, 2 rnds Cherry, rep from * once. Break working yarn in all colors.

Now, work a boomerang heel in stockinette stitch in Super White over the 32 sts of Ndls 4 and 1, following instructions on page 183.

Work the foot in stockinette stitch in the round over all sts on all 4 DPNs. *2 rnds Cherry, 2 rnds Super White, rep from * 11 times. Break working yarn in Cherry. Now, continue in stranded pattern from Chart B in Super White and Light Blue. Work Rnds

1–4 of chart once. Break the working yarn in Super White, and finish the sock in Light Blue. After 6.9 in. / 17.5 cm from middle of heel, start toe decreases.

Work paired banded toe decreases according to instructions on page 189. Break the working yarn, and pull the end through to the inside of the sock.

Weave in all ends.

Work the second sock the same way.

ANCHORS AWEIGH!

## WOMEN'S 5½/6
CO 64 sts (16 sts per needle).
Foot: *2 rnds Cherry, 2 rnds Super White, rep from * 9 times.
Now, follow Chart B, starting toe decreases 6.3 in. / 16 cm
from middle of heel.

## WOMEN'S 9/9½, MEN'S 7/7½
CO 68 sts (17 sts per needle).
Foot: *2 rnds Cherry, 2 rnds Super White, rep from * 12 times.
Now, follow Chart B, starting toe decreases 7.5 in. / 19 cm
from middle of heel.

## WOMEN'S 11/12, MEN'S 8½/9
CO 68 sts (17 sts per needle).
Foot: *2 rnds Cherry, 2 rnds Super White, rep from * 13 times.
Now, follow Chart B, starting toe decreases 8.1 in. / 20.5 cm
from middle of heel.

## MEN'S 10/11
CO 72 sts (18 sts per needle).
Foot: *2 rnds Cherry, 2 rnds Super White, rep from * 14 times.
Now, follow Chart B, starting toe decreases 8.7 in. / 22 cm
from middle of heel.

1. I'VE GOT YOUR NUMBER, SON
2. NEVER WANTED YOUR LOVE
3. BABY
4. I COULD'VE BEEN YOUR GIRL
5. TURN TO WHITE
6. SOMEBODY SWEET TO TALK TO
7. SOMETHING'S HAUNTING YOU
8. TOGETHER
9. HOLD ME, THRILL ME, KISS ME
10. SNOW QUEEN
11. SUNDAY GIRL
12. LONDON
13. SHADOW OF LOVE
14. REPRISE (I COULD'VE BEEN YOUR GIRL)

Kaffee →

Pause ←

&

Muted hues for putting

your feet up >>>>>>>>>>>

# SOXX NO. 20

## DIFFICULTY LEVEL 3

## SIZES

Women's 5½–Men's 11

Pattern instructions as given are for size Women's 7/8; changes to stitch counts and variations needed for the other sizes are given on page 125.

## YARN AND NEEDLES

Lang Yarns Jawoll; #1 fingering weight yarn; 75% wool, 25% nylon; 230 yd. / 210 m, 1.75 oz. / 50 g per skein; 1 skein each in #23 Light Grey Heathered, #70 Anthracite Heathered, and #150 Gold (For sizes Women's 11/12, Men's 8½/9 and up, you will need 2 skeins of Light Grey Heathered.)

DPN set of 5 needles in size US 1.5–2.5 / 2.5–3.0 mm

## GAUGE

In stranded pattern on US 1.5–2.5 / 2.5–3.0 mm needles 32 sts and 34 rnds = 4 × 4 in. / 10 × 10 cm

MUTED HUES FOR PUTTING YOUR FEET UP

## Stockinette Stitch
In rows: Knit on RS, purl on WS.
In rnds: Knit all sts in all rnds.

## Cuff Ribbing
Alternate "k1, p1."

## Colorwork Charts A and B
Stitch count has to be a multiple of 4.
Work all rnds in St st from the appropriate colorwork chart. Repeat the pattern repeat (4 sts wide) around.

### Colorwork Chart A

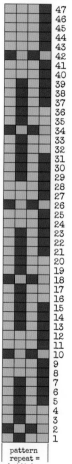

pattern repeat = 4 stitches

= Light Grey Heathered
= Anthracite Heathered
= Gold

### Colorwork Chart B

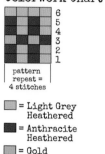

pattern repeat = 4 stitches

= Light Grey Heathered
= Anthracite Heathered
= Gold

MUTED HUES FOR PUTTING YOUR FEET UP

# INSTRUCTIONS

CO 64 sts in Light Grey Heathered, distribute evenly onto 4 DPNs (16 sts per needle), and join into round.

For the cuff, work 10 rnds (0.8 in. / 2 cm) in Cuff Ribbing pattern.

Work the leg in stockinette stitch, starting with 3 rnds Light Grey Heathered, then continue in stranded pattern from Chart A in Light Grey Heathered, Anthracite Heathered, and Gold. Work Rnds 1–47 of the chart once. Break the working yarn in Gold and Anthracite Heathered, and work another 5 rnds in Light Grey Heathered.

Now, work turned heel with heel flap in stockinette stitch in Light Grey Heathered over the 32 sts of Ndls 4 and 1 according to instructions on page 186.

Work the foot in stockinette stitch in the round over all sts of all 4 DPNs, starting with 20 rnds in Light Grey Heathered. Continue from Chart B in Light Grey Heathered, Anthracite Heathered, and Gold.

Work Rnds 1–6 of the chart 3 times. Break working yarn in Anthracite Heathered and Gold, continue in Light Grey Heathered. After 6.9 in. / 17.5 cm from middle of heel, start toe decreases.

Work toe with paired banded decreases in Light Grey Heathered, following instructions on page 189. Break the working yarn, and pull the end through to the inside of the sock.

Weave in all ends.

Work the second sock the same way.

MUTED HUES FOR PUTTING YOUR FEET UP

# STITCH COUNTS AND VARIATIONS FOR OTHER SIZES

**WOMEN'S 5½/6**
CO 64 sts (16 sts per needle).
Foot, Colorwork Chart B: Work Rnds 1–6 twice. Continue as stated in pattern, starting toe decreases 6.3 in. / 16 cm from middle of heel.

**WOMEN'S 9/9½, MEN'S 7/7½**
CO 68 sts (17 sts per needle).
Foot, Colorwork Chart B: Work Rnds 1–6 a total of 4 times. Continue as stated in pattern, starting toe decreases 7.5 in. / 19 cm from middle of heel.

**WOMEN'S 11/12, MEN'S 8½/9**
CO 68 sts (17 sts per needle).
Foot, Colorwork Chart B: Work Rnds 1–6 a total of 5 times. Continue as stated in pattern, starting toe decreases 8.1 in. / 20.5 cm from middle of heel.

**MEN'S 10/11**
CO 72 sts (18 sts per needle).
Foot, Colorwork Chart B: Work Rnds 1–6 a total 6 times. Continue as stated in pattern, starting toe decreases 8.7 in. / 22 cm from middle of heel.

# SOXX NO. 21

## DIFFICULTY LEVEL 2

## SIZES

Women's 9/9½, Men's 7/7½–Men's 12/13

Pattern instructions as given are for size Women's 11/12, Men's 8½/9; changes to stitch counts and variations needed for the other sizes are given on page 126.

## YARN AND NEEDLES

Schachenmayr Regia 4-ply; #1 fingering weight yarn; 75% wool, 25% polyamide; 230 yd. / 210 m, 1.75 oz. / 50 g or 460 yd. / 420 m, 3.5 oz. / 100 g per skein; one 1.75 oz. / 50 g skein in #522 Anthracite Heathered, and one 3.5 oz. / 100 g skein in #33 Flannel Streaked

DPN set of 5 needles in size US 1.5–2.5 / 2.5–3.0 mm

## GAUGE

In stranded pattern on US 1.5–2.5 / 2.5–3.0 mm needles 32 sts and 42 rnds = 4 × 4 in. / 10 × 10 cm

MUTED HUES FOR PUTTING YOUR FEET UP

## Stockinette Stitch

In rows: Knit on RS, purl on WS.
In rnds: Knit all sts in all rnds.

## Cuff Ribbing

Alternate "k1, p1."

## Colorwork Chart

Stitch count has to be a multiple of 4.
Work all rnds in St st from colorwork chart.
Repeat the pattern repeat (4 sts wide) around.

Colorwork Chart

4
3
2
1

pattern
repeat =
4 stitches

■ = Anthracite Heathered
□ = Flannel Streaked

# INSTRUCTIONS

CO 68 sts in Anthracite Heathered, distribute evenly onto 4 DPNs (17 sts per needle), and join into round.

For the cuff, work 10 rnds (1.2 in. / 3 cm) in Cuff Ribbing pattern.

Work first 10 rnds of leg in Anthracite Heathered in stockinette stitch, then continue in stranded pattern in Anthracite Heathered and Flannel Streaked. Work Rnds 1–4 of chart 10 times, then only Rnds 1–2 once. Break the working yarn in Anthracite Heathered and continue the leg in Flannel

MUTED HUES FOR PUTTING YOUR FEET UP

**WOMEN'S 9/9½, MEN'S 7/7½**
CO 68 sts (17 sts per needle).
Foot: After 7.5 in. / 19 cm from middle of heel, start toe decreases.

**MEN'S 10/11**
CO 72 sts (18 sts per needle).
Foot: After 8.7 in. / 22 cm from middle of heel, start toe decreases.

**MEN'S 12/13**
CO 76 sts (19 sts per needle).
Foot: After 9.3 in. / 23.5 cm from middle of heel, start toe decreases.

Streaked. After having reached an overall length of 7.5 in. / 19 cm, start turned heel with heel flap.
Work turned heel with heel flap in Flannel Streaked over the 34 sts of Ndls 4 and 1 according to instructions (see page 186).
Work the foot in the round over all sts on all 4 DPNs in stockinette stitch in Flannel Streaked. After 8.1 in. / 20.5 cm from middle of heel, start toe decreases.
Work toe with paired banded decreases in Flannel Streaked, following instructions on page 189. Break the working yarn, and pull the end through to the inside of the sock.
Weave in all ends.
Work the second sock the same way.

# SOXX NO.22

## DIFFICULTY LEVEL 3

## SIZES

Women's 5½–Men's 11

Pattern instructions as given are for size Women's 7/8; changes to stitch counts and variations needed for the other sizes are given on page 135.

## YARN AND NEEDLES

Lang Yarns Jawoll; #1 fingering weight yarn; 75% wool, 25% nylon; 230 yd. / 210 m, 1.75 oz. / 50 g per skein; 1 skein each in #01 White, #184 Azalea, #23 Light Grey Heathered, and #109 Pink

DPN set of 5 needles in size US 1.5–2.5 / 2.5–3.0 mm

## GAUGE

In stranded pattern on US 1.5–2.5 / 2.5–3.0 mm needles 34 sts and 38 rnds = 4 × 4 in. / 10 × 10 cm

MUTED HUES FOR PUTTING YOUR FEET UP

# Stockinette Stitch

In rows: Knit on RS, purl on WS.
In rnds: Knit all sts in all rnds.

## Cuff Ribbing

Alternate "k1, p1."

## Colorwork Charts A–D

Stitch count has to be a multiple of 4.
Work all rnds in St st from the appropriate colorwork chart. Repeat the pattern repeat (4 sts wide) around.

### Colorwork Chart A

4
3
2
1

pattern
repeat =
4 stitches

☐ = White
▨ = Azalea

### Colorwork Chart B

14
13
12
11
10
9
8
7
6
5
4
3
2
1

pattern
repeat =
4 stitches

☐ = White
▨ = Light Grey Heathered
▨ = Pink

### Colorwork Chart C

6
5
4
3
2
1

pattern
repeat =
4 stitches

☐ = White
▨ = Azalea

### Colorwork Chart D

6
5
4
3
2
1

pattern
repeat =
4 stitches

▨ = Light Grey Heathered
☐ = White
▨ = Pink

MUTED HUES FOR PUTTING YOUR FEET UP

# INSTRUCTIONS

CO 64 sts in Pink, distribute evenly onto 4 DPNs (16 sts per needle), and join into round.

For the cuff, work 12 rnds (1 in. / 2.5 cm) in Cuff Ribbing pattern. Break the working yarn in Pink.

Begin the leg with 1 rnd in stockinette stitch in White, then continue in stranded pattern from Chart A in White and Azalea. Work Rnds 1–4 of chart 10 times. Break the working yarn in Azalea. Now, continue in stranded pattern from Chart B in White, Light Grey Heathered, and Pink. Work Rnds 1–10 of the chart once. Break working yarn in all colors.

Now, work a boomerang heel in Light Grey Heathered in stockinette stitch over the 32 sts of Ndls 4 and 1, following instructions on page 183.

Work the foot in stockinette stitch in the round over all sts on all 4 DPNs in stranded pattern from Chart B in White, Light Grey Heathered, and Pink. Work Rnds 5–12 of the chart twice, then Rnds 13–14 once. Break the working yarn in Light Grey Heathered and Pink. Continue in stranded pattern C in White and Azalea. Work Rnds 1–6 of the chart 4 times, then only Rnds 1–3 once more. Break the working yarn in Azalea, then work in stranded pattern D in White, Light Grey Heathered, and Pink. Work Rnds 1–6 of the chart once. Break the working yarn in White and Light Grey Heathered, and finish the sock in Pink.

After 6.9 in. / 17.5 cm from middle of heel, start toe decreases.

Work toe with paired banded decreases in Pink, following instructions on page 189. Break the working yarn, and pull the end through to the inside of the sock.

Weave in all ends.

Work the second sock the same way.

MUTED HUES FOR PUTTING YOUR FEET UP

## STITCH COUNTS AND VARIATIONS FOR OTHER SIZES

### WOMEN'S 5½/6
CO 64 sts (16 sts per needle).
Foot, Colorwork Chart C: Work Rnds 1-6 of the chart 3 times, then only Rnds 1-3 once more. Continue as stated in pattern, starting toe decreases 6.3 in. / 16 cm from middle of heel.

### WOMEN'S 9/9½, MEN'S 7/7½
CO 68 sts (17 sts per needle).
Foot, Colorwork Chart C: Work Rnds 1-6 of the chart 4 times, then only Rnds 1-3 once more. Continue as stated in pattern, starting toe decreases 7.5 in. / 19 cm from middle of heel.

### WOMEN'S 11/12, MEN'S 8½/9
CO 68 sts (17 sts per needle).
Foot, Colorwork Chart C: Work Rnds 1-6 of the chart 5 times, then only Rnds 1-3 once more. Continue as stated in pattern, starting toe decreases 8.1 in. / 20.5 cm from middle of heel.

### MEN'S 10/11
CO 72 sts (18 sts per needle).
Foot, Colorwork Chart C: Work Rnds 1-6 of the chart 5 times, then only Rnds 1-3 once more. Continue as stated in pattern, starting toe decreases 8.7 in. / 22 cm from middle of heel.

# SOXX No. 23

## DIFFICULTY LEVEL 2

## SIZES

Women's 5½–Men's 11

Pattern instructions as given are for size Women's 7/8; changes to stitch counts and variations needed for the other sizes are given on page 139.

## YARN AND NEEDLES

Lang Yarns Jawoll; #1 fingering weight yarn; 75% wool, 25% nylon; 230 yd. / 210 m, 1.75 oz. / 50 g per skein; 1 skein each in #23 Light Grey Heathered and #159 Tangerine (For sizes Women's 11/12, Men's 8½/9 and up, you will need 2 skeins of Light Grey Heathered.)

DPN set of 5 needles in size US 1.5–2.5 / 2.5–3.0 mm

## GAUGE

In stranded pattern on US 1.5–2.5 / 2.5–3.0 mm needles
32 sts and 38 rnds = 4 × 4 in. / 10 × 10 cm

MUTED HUES FOR PUTTING YOUR FEET UP

## Stockinette Stitch

In rows: Knit on RS, purl on WS.
In rnds: Knit all sts in all rnds.

## Cuff Ribbing

Alternate "k1, p1."

## Colorwork Charts A and B

Stitch count has to be a multiple of 4.
Work all rnds in St st from the appropriate colorwork chart. Repeat the pattern repeat (4 sts wide) around.

# INSTRUCTIONS

CO 64 sts in Tangerine, distribute evenly onto 4 DPNs (16 sts per needle), and join into round.

For the cuff, work 3 rnds in Tangerine and 10 rnds in Light Grey Heathered (1 in. / 2.5 cm) in Cuff Ribbing pattern.

Begin the leg with 10 rnds in Light Grey Heathered in stockinette stitch, then continue in stranded pattern from Chart A in Light Grey Heathered and Tangerine. Work Rnds 1–29 of the chart once. Break working yarn in Tangerine, and work another 10 rnds in Light Grey Heathered.

Now, work a boomerang heel in Light Grey Heathered in stockinette stitch over the 32 sts of Ndls 4 and 1, following instructions on page 183.

Work the foot in stockinette stitch in the round over all sts of all 4 DPNs. First, work 9 rnds in Light Grey Heathered then continue in stranded pattern B in Light Grey Heathered and Tangerine. Work Rnds 1–8 of the chart 4 times. Break working yarn in Tangerine, and continue in Light Grey Heathered. After 6.9 in. / 17.5 cm from middle of heel, start toe decreases.

Work toe with paired banded decreases in Light Grey Heathered, following instructions on page 189. Break the working yarn, and pull the end through to the inside of the sock.

Weave in all ends.

Work the second sock the same way.

Colorwork Chart A

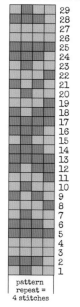

pattern
repeat =
4 stitches

▢ = Light Grey Heathered
▨ = Tangerine

Colorwork Chart B

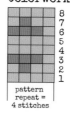

pattern
repeat =
4 stitches

▢ = Light Grey Heathered
▨ = Tangerine

# STITCH COUNTS AND VARIATIONS FOR OTHER SIZES

**WOMEN'S 5½/6**
CO 64 sts (16 sts per needle).
Foot, Colorwork Chart B: Work Rnds 1–8 a total of 3 times,
starting toe decreases 6.3 in. / 16 cm from middle of heel.

**WOMEN'S 9/9½, MEN'S 7/7½**
CO 68 sts (17 sts per needle).
Foot, Colorwork Chart B: Work Rnds 1–8 a total of 5 times,
starting toe decreases 7.5 in. / 19 cm from middle of heel.

**WOMEN'S 11/12, MEN'S 8½/9**
CO 68 sts (17 sts per needle).
Foot, Colorwork Chart B: Work Rnds 1–8 a total of 5 times,
starting toe decreases 8.1 in. / 20.5 cm from middle of heel.

**MEN'S 10/11**
CO 72 sts (18 sts per needle).
Foot, Colorwork Chart B: Work Rnds 1–8 a total of 6 times,
starting toe decreases 8.7 in. / 22 cm from middle of heel.

# SOXX NO. 24+25

### DIFFICULTY LEVEL 1

### SIZES

Women's 5½–Men's 11

Pattern instructions as given are for size Women's 7/8; changes to stitch counts and variations needed for the other sizes are given on page 143.

### YARN AND NEEDLES (FOR 2 PAIRS OF SOCKS)

Schoppel ALB Lino; #1 super fine weight yarn; 438 yd. / 400 m, 3.5 oz. / 100 g per skein; 1 skein each in #3285 Claret and #9200 Semi-Solid Mid-Grey

DPN set of 5 needles in size US 2.5–6 / 3.0–4.0 mm

### GAUGE

In stockinette stitch on US 2.5–6 / 3.0–4.0 mm needles 28 sts and 40 rnds = 4 × 4 in. / 10 × 10 cm

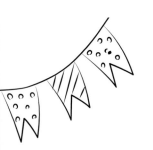

MUTED HUES FOR PUTTING YOUR FEET UP

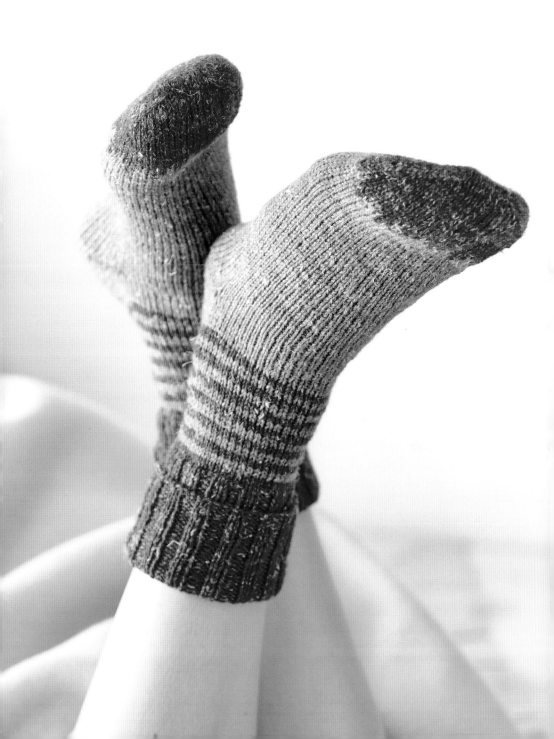

## Stockinette Stitch
In rows: Knit on RS, purl on WS.
In rnds: Knit all sts in all rnds.

## Cuff Ribbing
Alternate "k2, p2."

## Colorwork Chart
Stitch count has to be a multiple of 4.
Work all rnds in St st from colorwork chart.
    Repeat the pattern repeat (4 sts wide)
    around.

Colorwork Chart

| | 4 |
| | 3 |
| | 2 |
| | 1 |

pattern
repeat =
4 stitches

■ = Semi-Solid Mid-Grey
■ = Claret

# INSTRUCTIONS SOXX #24

CO 56 sts in Semi-Solid Mid-Grey, distribute
    evenly onto 4 DPNs (14 sts per needle),
    and join into round.
For the cuff, work 50 rnds (4.7 in. / 12 cm) in
    Cuff Ribbing pattern.
Begin the leg in stockinette stitch with 14
    rnds in Semi-Solid Mid-Grey. Now, contin-
    ue in stranded pattern in Semi-Solid Mid-
    Grey and Claret. Work Rnds 1–4 of chart
    once. Break the working yarn in Semi-Solid
    Mid-Grey, and work 10 rnds in Claret.
Work a boomerang heel in Claret over the 28
    sts of Ndls 4 and 1 according to instruc-
    tions on page 183.
Continue the foot in Claret in stockinette
    stitch in the round over all sts of all 4
    DPNs. After 6.7 in. / 17 cm from middle of
    heel, begin stripes, alternating 2 rnds
    Semi-Solid Mid-Grey and 2 rnds Claret.
    Continue the stripe pattern to the end,
    starting decreases for the rounded toe
    after 8 in. / 20 cm from middle of heel.
Work rounded toe according to instructions
    on page 189. Graft the remaining opening
    in Kitchener stitch (see page 190).
Weave in all ends. Fold the cuff over.
Work the second sock the same way.

# STITCH COUNTS AND VARIATIONS FOR OTHER SIZES

## WOMEN'S 5½/6
CO 56 sts (14 sts per needle).
Foot: After 6.1 in. / 15.5 cm from middle of heel, begin stripes, alternating 2 rnds Semi-Solid Mid-Grey and 2 rnds Claret. Continue stripe pattern to end, starting decreases for the rounded toe 7.3 in. / 18.5 cm from middle of heel.

## WOMEN'S 9/9½, MEN'S 7/7½
CO 60 sts (15 sts per needle).
Foot: After 7.3 in. / 18.5 cm from middle of heel, begin stripes, alternating 2 rnds Semi-Solid Mid-Grey and 2 rnds Claret. Continue stripe pattern to end, starting decreases for the rounded toe after 8.5 in. / 21.5 cm from middle of heel.

## WOMEN'S 11/12, MEN'S 8½/9
CO 60 sts (15 sts per needle).
Foot: After 8 in. / 20 cm from middle of heel, begin stripes, alternating 2 rnds Semi-Solid Mid-Grey and 2 rnds Claret. Continue stripe pattern to end, starting decreases for the rounded toe after 9.1 in. / 23 cm from middle of heel.

## MEN'S 10/11
CO 64 sts (16 sts per needle).
Foot: After 8.5 in. / 21.5 cm from middle of heel, begin stripes, alternating 2 rnds Semi-Solid Mid-Grey and 2 rnds Claret. Continue stripe pattern to end, starting decreases for the rounded toe after 9.6 in. / 24.5 cm from middle of heel.

# INSTRUCTIONS SOXX #25

CO 56 sts in Claret, distribute evenly onto 4 DPNs (14 sts per needle), and join into round.

For the cuff, work 50 rnds (4.7 in. / 12 cm) in Cuff Ribbing pattern.

Work the leg in stockinette stitch. For this, work *2 rnds Claret, 2 rnds Semi-Solid Mid-Grey, rep from * 6 times. Break the working yarn in Claret. Work another 3 rnds in Semi-Solid Mid-Grey.

Now, work a boomerang heel in Semi-Solid Mid-Grey over the 28 sts of Ndls 4 and 1, following instructions on page 183.

Continue the foot in Semi-Solid Mid-Grey in stockinette stitch in the round over all sts of all 4 DPNs. After 6.7 in. / 17 cm from middle of heel, continue in stranded pattern in Claret and Semi-Solid Mid-Grey. Work Rnds 1–4 of chart once. Break the working yarn in Semi-Solid Mid-Grey, and finish the sock in Claret. After 8 in. / 20 cm from middle of heel, start decreases for the rounded toe.

Work rounded toe according to instructions on page 189. Graft the remaining opening in Kitchener stitch (see page 190).

Weave in all ends. Fold half of the cuff over to the right side.

Work the second sock the same way.

MUTED HUES FOR PUTTING YOUR FEET UP

# STITCH COUNTS AND VARIATIONS FOR OTHER SIZES

## WOMEN'S 5½/6
CO 56 sts (14 sts per needle).
Foot: After 6.1 in. / 15.5 cm from middle of heel, work stranded colorwork in Claret and Semi-Solid Mid-Grey. Work Rnds 1–4 once. Continue as stated in pattern, starting decreases for the rounded toe after 7.3 in. / 18.5 cm from middle of heel.

## WOMEN'S 9/9½, MEN'S 7/7½
CO 60 sts (15 sts per needle).
Foot: After 7.3 in. / 18.5 cm from middle of heel, work stranded colorwork in Claret and Semi-Solid Mid-Grey. Work Rnds 1–4 once. Continue as stated in pattern, starting decreases for the rounded toe after 8.5 in. / 21.5 cm from middle of heel.

## WOMEN'S 11/12, MEN'S 8½/9
CO 60 sts (15 sts per needle).
Foot: After 8 in. / 20 cm from middle of heel, work stranded colorwork in Claret and Semi-Solid Mid-Grey. Work Rnds 1–4 once. Continue as stated in pattern, starting decreases for the rounded toe after 9 in. / 23 cm from middle of heel.

## MEN'S 10/11
CO 64 sts (16 sts per needle).
Foot: After 8.5 in. / 21.5 cm from middle of heel, work stranded colorwork in Claret and Semi-Solid Mid-Grey. Work Rnds 1–4 once. Continue as stated in pattern, starting decreases for the rounded toe after 9.6 in. / 24.5 cm from middle of heel.

# SOXX NO. 26

## DIFFICULTY LEVEL 3

### SIZES

Women's 5½–Men's 11

Pattern instructions as given are for size Women's 7/8; changes to stitch counts and variations needed for the other sizes are given on page 151.

### YARN AND NEEDLES

Lang Yarns Jawoll; #1 fingering weight yarn; 75% wool, 25% nylon; 230 yd. / 210 m, 1.75 oz. / 50 g per skein; 1 skein each in #23 Light Grey Heathered, #70 Anthracite Heathered, and #219 Pink

DPN set of 5 needles in size US 1.5–2.5 / 2.5–3.0 mm

### GAUGE

In stranded pattern on US 1.5–2.5 / 2.5–3.0 mm needles 32 sts and 36 rnds = 4 × 4 in. / 10 × 10 cm

MUTED HUES FOR PUTTING YOUR FEET UP

## Colorwork Charts A and B

Stitch count has to be a multiple of 4.

Work all rnds in St st from the appropriate colorwork chart. Repeat the pattern repeat (4 sts wide) around.

### Colorwork Chart A

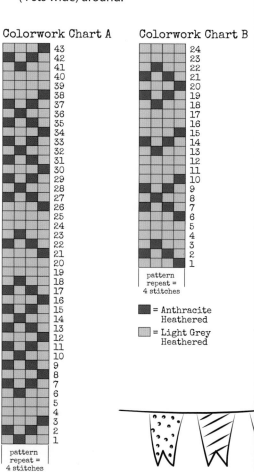

43
42
41
40
39
38
37
36
35
34
33
32
31
30
29
28
27
26
25
24
23
22
21
20
19
18
17
16
15
14
13
12
11
10
9
8
7
6
5
4
3
2
1

pattern
repeat =
4 stitches

■ = Light Grey Heathered
■ = Anthracite Heathered

### Colorwork Chart B

24
23
22
21
20
19
18
17
16
15
14
13
12
11
10
9
8
7
6
5
4
3
2
1

pattern
repeat =
4 stitches

■ = Anthracite Heathered
□ = Light Grey Heathered

## Stockinette Stitch

In rows: Knit on RS, purl on WS.
In rnds: Knit all sts in all rnds.

## Cuff Ribbing

Alternate "k1, p1."

# INSTRUCTIONS

CO 64 sts in Light Grey Heathered, distribute evenly onto 4 DPNs (16 sts per needle), and join into round.

For the cuff, work 10 rnds in Light Grey Heathered and 4 rnds in Pink (1.2 in. / 3.0 cm) in Cuff Ribbing pattern. Break the working yarn in Pink.

Work the leg in stockinette stitch, beginning with 2 rnds Light Grey Heathered. Now, continue in stranded pattern A in Anthracite Heathered and Light Grey Heathered. Work Rnds 1–43 of the chart once. Break working yarn in both colors.

Work a boomerang heel in stockinette stitch in Pink over the 32 sts of Ndls 4 and 1, following instructions on page 183. Now, break the working yarn.

Work the foot in stockinette stitch in the round over all sts of all 4 DPNs, beginning with 2 rnds in Light Grey Heathered. Continue in stranded pattern B in Anthracite Heathered and Light Grey Heathered. Work Rnds 1–24 of the chart once, then only Rnds 1–17 once more. Break the working yarn in Light Grey Heathered and in Anthracite Heathered. Continue in

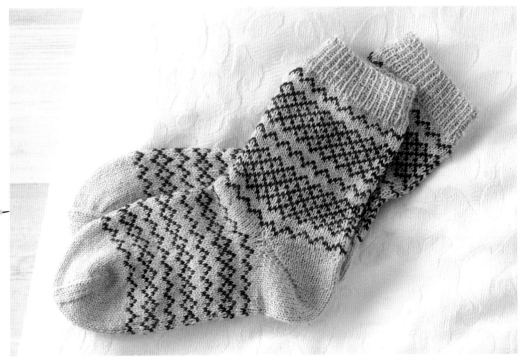

stockinette stitch in Pink, starting toe decreases after 6.9 in. / 17.5 cm from middle of heel.

Work toe with paired banded decreases in Pink according to instructions on page 189.

Break the working yarn, and pull the end through to the inside of the sock.

Weave in all ends.

Work the second sock the same way.

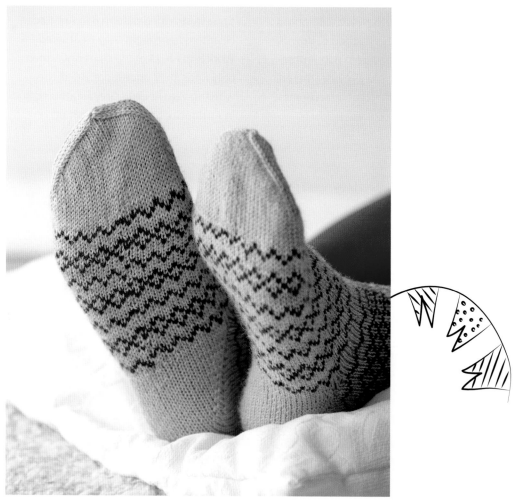

**WOMEN'S 5½/6**
CO 64 sts (16 sts per needle).
Foot, Colorwork Chart B: Work Rnds 1–24 once, then work only Rnds 1–12 once. Continue as stated in pattern, starting toe decreases 6.3 in. / 16 cm from middle of heel.

**WOMEN'S 9/9½, MEN'S 7/7½**
CO 68 sts (17 sts per needle).
Foot, Colorwork Chart B: Work Rnds 1–24 twice. Continue as stated in pattern, starting toe decreases 7.5 in. / 19 cm from middle of heel.

**WOMEN'S 11/12, MEN'S 8½/9**
CO 68 sts (17 sts per needle).
Foot, Colorwork Chart B: Work Rnds 1–24 twice, then work only Rnds 1–5 once. Continue as stated in pattern, starting toe decreases 8.1 in. / 20.5 cm from middle of heel.

**MEN'S 10/11**
CO 72 sts (18 sts per needle).
Foot, Colorwork Chart B: Work Rnds 1–24 twice, then work only Rnds 1–12 once. Continue as stated in pattern, starting toe decreases 8.7 in. / 22 cm from middle of heel.

Getting creative with

sock design >>>>>>>>>>>

# DESIGN YOUR OWN SOCKS

You've found your favorite sock but want to knit it in different colors? No problem! Sock yarn is offered in a wide variety of colorways. Options for inspiration can be found on pages 152–153.

Calm, neutral colorways, such as white, off-white, light grey, or beige, are ideal as main colors, ensuring that even a lively color-work pattern won't look too loud. Patterns can be worked in a tonal color scheme, for instance, in different shades of blue, or in a color mix. Two-color patterns will look completely different if the main and contrasting colors are switched.

If using just two or three colors for an originally multicolored pattern, the result is a completely new design.

Since the pattern repeat for all patterns in this book is always 4 stitches wide, you can combine stitch patterns from different socks for a new look. The cuff can be worked longer, or the leg portion shorter, resulting in your very own design, with endless possibilities for pretty socks.

I design my patterns either on paper (using a pencil or colored pencils) or on the computer. In Excel, it's easy to create patterns, quickly modify them, and view various color combinations. To create a colorwork grid, set the column width to 0.9 points and the row height to 7.25 points, which creates square-shaped cells, waiting to be filled with background color by you.

Sometimes, I just start knitting without a plan, which is especially exciting and often produces the most beautiful patterns. When doing this, I frequently use leftover yarns from my remnant basket.

For many ideas, I find inspiration online, such as on Instagram and Pinterest. What gives me ideas for a new sock design is not always knitwear. Colored illustrations, graphic patterns from the home decor sector, and beautiful dishware are my biggest source of ideas.

To my chagrin, knitting magazines don't publish sock patterns very often. However, stitch patterns from sweaters, cardigans, and other knitwear can be easily adapted for socks if the pattern repeat is compatible with the cast-on number. Fabric designers often create stunning patterns in very intense colors—the color combinations from these serve as inspiration for especially colorful socks.

Since the Baltic Sea is practically right at my front door, maritime-themed socks are a staple of mine. They pair wonderfully with denim jeans and striped tops, and can be worn during the summer too. When the occasion calls for something subtler, I prefer socks patterned in greys and beiges. Only in rare cases will I venture out in black socks with simple knit-purl patterns.

SOXX no.9 from page 58, worked in Lang Yarns Jawoll in #184 Azalea, #159 Tangerine, #43 Yellow, and #01 White.

SOXX no.5 from page 32, worked in Schachenmayr Regia 4-ply in #2080 Super White, #2041 Yellow, and #44 Mid-Grey Streaked.

SOXX no. 23 from page 136, worked in Lang Yarns Jawoll in #70 Anthracite Heathered and #150 Gold.

SOXX no.6 from page 38, worked in Lang Yarns Jawoll in #23 Light Grey Heathered, #25 Navy, and #61 Burgundy.

SOXX no. 8
from page 52,
worked in Lang
Yarns Jawoll in #01
White, #60 Red, and
#25 Navy.

GETTING CREATIVE WITH SOCK DESIGN

SOXX NO. 1 from page 10, worked in Schachenmayr Regia 4-ply in #2080 Super White, #33 Flannel Streaked, #17 Light Camel Streaked, and #522 Anthracite Heathered.

SOXX No.7 from page 46, worked in Lang Yarns Jawoll in #290 Eggplant.

GETTING CREATIVE WITH SOCK DESIGN

SOXX no.21 from page 126, worked in Lang Yarns Jawoll in #184 Azalea and #23 Light Grey Heathered.

163

sock yarn

reinforcement
thread

stitch
markers

needle gauge

tape measure

scissors

tapestry
needle

Sock basics

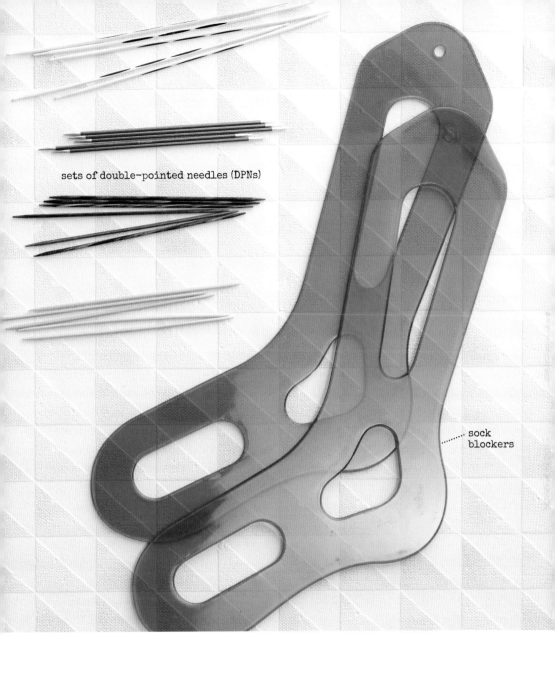

sets of double-pointed needles (DPNs)

sock
blockers

# MATERIALS

## YARN

Socks should always be knit from yarns marketed specifically as sock yarns, which are usually a blend of wool combined with about 25–30% polyamide (nylon). Fiber content and special treatment make this blend hard-wearing as well as machine washable without felting.

Socks in stranded patterns are best worked from 4-ply yarns with a yardage of about 230 yd. / 210 m per 1.75 oz. / 50 g. With yarns thicker than that, more elaborate stranded patterns can prove too bulky in the instep area. Textured patterns from knit and purl stitches, other single-color patterns, or stripes are a good choice for the thicker 6-ply yarn weights. Leftover yarns by different manufacturers may be combined into one project without problems, as long as they are of comparable fiber content and yarn weight.

When using thinner yarns, heel and toe can be supplemented with reinforcement thread in the same color, which is often sold along with the main yarn.

Sock yarns also come in pure natural fibers without synthetic additions. ALB Lino yarn by Schoppel, used for SoXX #4, SoXX #7, and SoXX #24 & 25 in this book, is a blend of 85% wool and 15% linen.

Make sure to choose a high-quality yarn to be able to enjoy your socks for a long time to come.

## KNITTING NEEDLES

There are various techniques for knitting socks. Traditionally, DPN sets of 5 needles are used, which are available in different materials, shapes, and lengths. Whether to use wood, steel, plastic, or bamboo needles depends entirely on personal preference. When deciding on a material, personal gauge (how tightly or loosely one knits) is an important factor.

Bamboo needles are wonderfully lightweight and very yielding during knitting. Their grippy surface makes stitches less likely to slip off but makes them at the same time less suitable for very tight knitters.

Steel needles are somewhat heavier than needles made from other materials and have the big advantage that they don't break.

However, because of their much slicker surface, they are prone to sliding out of the knitting when working very loosely.

Wooden needles are pleasantly smooth and also lightweight. Sets in smaller sizes often contain a sixth needle, meant as a replacement in case one of the others should break.

Plastic needles are lightweight too, plus they are flexible. Their tips are more rounded, which makes them less suitable for knitting with multiple colors.

Nowadays, needles are also manufactured in different cross-sectional shapes. Choices include traditional round, triangular, or square-shaped needles.

When it comes to needle length, a wide range is offered too. For socks, needles with a length of 6 in. / 15 cm are best suited.

## NOTIONS

Other tools needed are a tape measure to determine the correct foot length, scissors, and a dull tapestry needle for grafting the toe seam, as well as for hiding ends.

Stitch markers and row counters make work easier but are not essential. A homemade little loop from a piece of contrasting yarn or a piece of paper and pencil will do too.

To prevent stitches from sliding off the needles while on the move with a knitting project, specialized stores offer DPN set holders, endcaps, and DPN tubes. Of course, rubber bands may be used just as well to hold your DPNs together.

When DPN sets of various sizes have accumulated, a needle gauge comes in handy to assemble a set of needles in the appropriate size required for a project.

# KNITTING BASICS

## LONG-TAIL CAST-ON

For socks, I recommend the classic long-tail cast-on, since this cast-on method is elastic but not too loose.

**1.** Unwind about 24 to 28 in. / 60 to 70 cm of yarn, make a beginning loop or slip-knot onto a needle, and tighten it.

**2.** Lead the yarn tail over your thumb, and the working yarn connected to the ball over the outstretched index finger. The needle with the slipknot is between both fingers. Grasp both yarn ends with the free fingers of your left hand to pull them taut.

**3.** Now, insert the needle from front to back underneath the strand of yarn in front, and using the tip of the needle, pull the strand of yarn from your index finger through from the back to the front. Let the stitch slide off the thumb. Using your thumb, grasp the working yarn again and pull through to the front. This tightens the stitch, and the yarn goes again over the thumb.

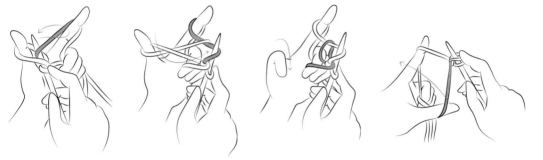

**4.** Repeat these steps until you've cast on the required stitch count, evenly distributing the total amount of stitches onto four needles. When transitioning to the next needle, keep the yarn taut. Before joining into the round, make sure your cast-on round is not twisted.

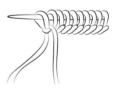

# KNIT STITCH

Hold the needle bearing the cast-on stitches in your left hand and the working needle in the right hand, with the working yarn behind the needle. Lead the working yarn over the outstretched index finger of the left hand. It can be tightened by winding it several times around the index finger or the pinkie finger.

**1.** To form a stitch, insert the working needle from front to back into the center of the first stitch, and pull the working yarn through the loop from back to front.

**2.** Tighten the newly formed stitch on the right needle, and let the stitch of the previous row or round slide from the left needle.

**3.** Work the following stitches the same way.

PLEASE NOTE: Left-handed knitters hold the needle bearing the cast-on stitches in the right hand, and the working needle in their left hand.

# PURL STITCH

As with the knit stitch, the needle bearing the cast-on stitches is held in your left hand, and the working needle in the right hand. Before a purl stitch, the working yarn needs to be brought to the front of the work.

**1.** With the tip of the right needle in front of the left needle, insert the working needle into the center of the first stitch from right to left, and pull the working yarn through the stitch from front to back.

**2.** Tighten the newly formed stitch on the right needle, and let the stitch of the previous row or round slide from the left needle.

**3.** Work the following stitches the same way.

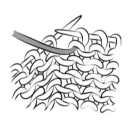  

PLEASE NOTE: Left-handed knitters hold the needle bearing the cast-on stitches in their right, and the working needle in their left hand.

BY THE WAY: Since in Eastern European as well as in Islamic countries the working yarn is pulled through the stitch in the opposite direction, knit stitches are mounted on the needle with the other leg in front. This is especially important when working right- or left-leaning decreases. With this way of creating stitches, holes are unavoidable when working a boomerang heel.

# STITCHES WORKED THROUGH THE BACK LOOP

## KNITTING THROUGH THE BACK LOOP

Insert the needle from right to left into the back leg of the stitch, and knit the stitch, creating a twisted knit stitch.

## PURLING THROUGH THE BACK LOOP

Insert the needle from left to right into the back leg of the stitch, and purl the stitch, creating a twisted purl stitch.

# GERMAN SHORT ROWS WITH DOUBLE STITCH

After RS rows as well as after WS rows, turn work and bring the working yarn to the front of the work. Slip the first stitch unworked, at the same time pulling the working yarn away from you until taut. The stitch is pulled over the needle, with its two legs now sitting on the needle.

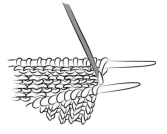  

# YARN OVER

A yarn over is created by leading the working yarn around the right needle from front to back before working the next stitch. While doing so, the working yarn is pulled to the back not too tightly.

# DECREASES

## KNITTING 2 STITCHES TOGETHER

In the knitted fabric, this decrease leans to the right.

Insert the right needle knitwise into the two following stitches at the same time. Grasp the working yarn, pulling it through both stitches at once.

## SLIP-KNIT-PASS

In the knitted fabric, this decrease leans to the left.

Insert the right needle knitwise into the following stitch, and slip the stitch onto the right needle. Knit the next stitch, and pass the slipped stitch over the knitted one.

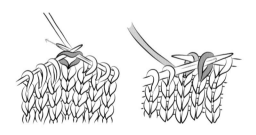

## SLIP-SLIP-KNIT

Another way of making a left-leaning decrease is to slip-slip-knit. For this, slip one stitch knitwise. Now, slip the next stitch knitwise too. Insert the left needle from left to right into both slipped stitches at the same time, grasp the working yarn, and pull it through both stitches.

# THE SOCK

## TURNED HEEL WITH ROUNDED TOE

Cuff

Toe decreases·

Rounded toe

INSTEP

mid heel to start of toe decreases

LEG

SOLE

heel flap

gusset

heel turn

# BOOMERANG HEEL WITH PAIRED BANDED TOE DECREASES

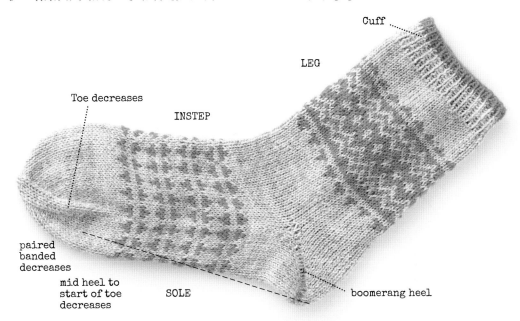

Cuff

LEG

Toe decreases

INSTEP

paired
banded
decreases

mid heel to
start of toe
decreases

SOLE

boomerang heel

## SIZE CHART

If not otherwise stated, given for 4-ply fingering weight (yardage 230 yd. / 1.75 oz [210 m / 50 g])

| Size | W5½/6 | W7/8 | W9/9½, M7/7½ | W11/12, M8½/9 | M10/11 | M12/13 |
|---|---|---|---|---|---|---|
| Cast on/sts per needle | | | | | | |
| Stranded pattern | 64/16 | 64/16 | 68/17 | 68/17 | 72/18 | 76/19 |
| Textured patterns in knit and purl, stripes etc. | 60/15 | 60/15 | 64/16 | 64/16 | 68/17 | 72/18 |
| ALB Lino by Schoppel or similar weight yarn (yardage 437.5 yd. / 3.5 oz. [400 m / 100 g]) | 56/14 | 56/14 | 60/15 | 60/15 | 64/16 | 68/17 |
| Paired decreases: foot length in in. [cm] from mid heel to start of toe decreases | 6.3 [16] | 6.9 [17.5] | 7.5 [19] | 8.1 [20.5] | 8.7 [22] | 9.3 [23.5] |
| Rounded toe: foot length in in. [cm] from mid heel to start of toe decreases | 7.3 [18.5] | 7.9 [20] | 8.3 [21.5] | 9.1 [23] | 9.7 [24.5] | 10.2 [26] |
| Total foot length in in. [cm] | 8.3 [21.5] | 9.1 [23] | 9.7 [24.5] | 10.2 [26] | 10.8 [27.5] | 11.4 [29] |

175

# THE PERFECT SIZE

How many stitches to cast on to end up with a well-fitting sock depends on various parameters—on the one hand, the yarn weight used, the foot size, and the gauge, and on the other, also the foot circumference.

Every foot is different. With narrow, long feet, it can happen that fewer stitches need to be cast on than are listed for the indicated size. Similarly, for short, wide feet, most likely more stitches will need to be cast on than are stated for the actual size. For the patterns in this book, this presents no problem at all since all pattern repeats are 4 stitches wide, enabling you to switch out stitch counts from smaller or larger sizes.

Stranded patterns can be adapted individually to match the foot length too—just work fewer or more pattern repeats. If you are not sure, try on your sock-in-progress to check the length.

The leg of the sock can be individually adapted by extending or shortening the colorwork pattern.

# GAUGE

You might be used to preparing a gauge swatch as a flat piece of about 4.7 × 4.7 in. / 12 × 12 cm worked in stockinette stitch, which includes purling the wrong-side rows for stranded colorwork patterns. This is rather tedious, plus the gauge swatch might not exactly match a piece worked in the round. For this reason, I recommend swatching in the round.

With this method, instead of counting the stitches per 4 in. / 10 cm, you measure only 2 in. / 5 cm and double the stitch count.

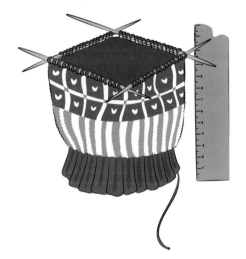

If your gauge swatch has more stitches than stated in the pattern gauge, you've knitted too tightly and need to switch to a larger needle size. If you have fewer stitches and your swatch is rather loosely knitted, you need to use a smaller needle size. Specialized stores will carry needle sizes in 0.01 in. / 0.25 mm increments.

The gauge for a stranded pattern will, as a rule, turn out tighter than the one for pieces worked in just one color. For patterns containing one section in a stranded pattern and another one in a solid color (such as SoX #12), different needle sizes can be used to adjust for the discrepancy. The stranded pattern may be worked with a larger needle size than the section in one color.

Stranded patterns are less elastic than solid colors, making it necessary to cast on more stitches than for socks worked in one color only.

# CUFF AND LEG

## CUFF

The cuff's purpose is not only to hold up the sock; it can also be a decorative element.

Ribbed cuffs can be worked in different ways. The two most common ones are 1 × 1 and 2 × 2 ribbing. For cuffs in 1 × 1 ribbing, the stitch count has to be a multiple of 2. After the cast-on, all rounds are worked alternating "k1, p1" until the desired cuff length has been reached.

For a cuff in 2 × 2 ribbing, the stitch count has to be a multiple of 4. After the cast-on, rounds are worked alternating "k2, p2."

An especially pretty and very elastic cuff is created when the knit stitches are worked through the back loop (tbl). Since this type of fabric will constrict more, the stitch columns are more pronounced. After the cast-on, rounds are worked alternating "k1-tbl, p1."

Different cuff ribbings can be chosen according to personal preferences, and the cuff length can be changed as desired as well.

## LEG

After the cuff follows the leg, which for socks in stranded patterns is worked in stockinette stitch in the round. It is worked as a straight tube, without increases or decreases. For most socks, the leg length can be varied freely. Socks for the summer are often shorter, while classic winter socks have a longer leg.

# STRANDED COLORWORK TECHNIQUE

Knitting stranded colorwork needs a little bit of practice and patience but is well worth the effort. With this technique, gorgeous and colorful customized socks can be created.

## KNITTING TENSION

Stranded patterns are worked using two or more colors in every round, following a colorwork chart. While working in one color, the unused color is carried along in the back of the work. Even tension should be held throughout.

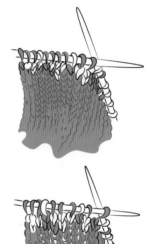

If the unused color in the back is pulled too taut, the knitted fabric will constrict. Should this happen, it might be necessary to pull the stitches longer before a color change, or to switch to a larger needle size.

When the float in the unused color is too loose, the knitted fabric will look untidy, and gaps between stitches in different colors may show. In this case, it might help to use a smaller needle size.

To prevent unsightly laddering at the transition, proper tension is especially important in the spots where one needle ends and the next one starts. In these places, pull the working yarn tighter than usual.

For the patterns in this book, the second color is never carried over more than 3 stitches in the back of the work, which eliminates the need for locking in floats and keeps the fabric more elastic—the more frequently an unused color is woven in, the less elastic the knitted fabric will turn out.

If a color stays unused for several rounds, the yarn in this color needs to be crossed with the current color after the third or fourth round of inactivity. This prevents vertical loops on the inside, which could get caught when pulling on and taking off the socks. Here, too, make sure to pull the yarn upward not too tightly.

## HOLDING THE WORKING YARN

There are different ways of holding the yarn. I hold it leading both strands up over the index finger of my left hand. To achieve the correct tension, the front yarn goes down in front of and the back yarn behind the middle finger, after which both yarns are held in place with the ring finger and pinkie finger of the same hand. Left-handed knitters need to lead the yarns over their right index finger accordingly.

It is important to always keep the same color as the front yarn, since switching between front and back yarns will be noticeable, causing an unruly stitch appearance.

The white yarn is in front of the red one.

The red yarn is in front of the white strand.

# HOW TO READ A COLORWORK OR KNITTING SYMBOL CHART

Colorwork charts and knitting symbol charts are read from bottom to top and from right to left. The pattern repeat is repeated all the way around. One box corresponds to one stitch, and one chart row equals one round in the knitted piece.

As an example, see the zigzag pattern from SoX #1.

### Colorwork Chart

4
3
2
1

pattern
repeat =
4 stitches

☐ = Off-White
▨ = Tangerine

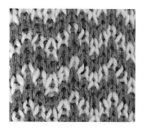

The pattern starts with 1 stitch in Off-White, followed by 1 stitch in Tangerine and then 2 more stitches in Off-White. After the fourth stitch, the pattern repeat starts anew, again working 1 stitch in Off-White, and after that, 1 stitch in Tangerine, and so forth. It is important to note that the pattern repeat is 4 stitches wide; accordingly, the overall stitch count has to be a multiple of 4.

The instructions state that the colorwork chart needs to be worked 9 times, which means to start from Round 1 again after completion of Round 4, as often as needed until the zigzag pattern has been worked the required number of times.

For socks with textured instead of colorwork patterns, a symbol chart is followed the same way.

A round always begins with the first stitch of the first needle and ends with the last stitch of the fourth needle. In the finished sock, the beginning of the round falls either in the center back of the sock or in the middle of the sole.

# HEEL

## BOOMERANG HEEL OR TURNED HEEL WITH HEEL FLAP?

In many socks, the heel can be switched to a different type, depending on personal preferences. A boomerang heel can be easily added to any sock. When the foot starts with a stranded color-work pattern, however, a turned heel can only be added with additional adjustments to the sock. The colorwork patterns in this book do not include incorporated gusset decreases. Of the patterns in this book worked with a boomerang heel only SoX #15 could be worked alternatively with a turned heel, since the sole has its own pattern.

## BOOMERANG HEEL

Boomerang heels are worked using the German short rows method with double stitch. To make the double stitch: turn the work and bring the working yarn to the front of the work; slip the first stitch unworked, at the same time pulling the working yarn away from you until taut. The stitch is pulled over the needle, with its two legs now sitting on the needle.

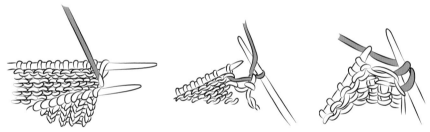

For the boomerang heel, work over the stitches of the fourth and first needle in stockinette stitch. For this, combine all stitches onto one needle, and divide them into 3 parts, using stitch markers between sections (see tables on page 185).

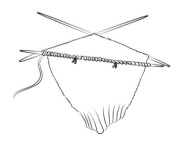

In the **first (upper)** part of the heel, you work over the stitches between the two double stitches only, always turning before the previous double stitch, as follows:

**Row 1 (RS):** Knit all sts, turn.

**Row 2 (WS):** Slip 1 st with yarn in front and pull a double stitch, purl all other sts, turn.

**Row 3 (RS):** Slip 1 st with yarn in front and pull out a double stitch, knit to double stitch, turn.

**Row 4 (WS):** Slip 1 st with yarn in front and pull out a double stitch, purl to double stitch, turn.

Repeat Rows 3 and 4 until all stitches in the first and last thirds are double stitches; all stitches in the middle third should be single stitches.

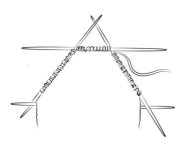

Now, knit for 2 rounds over all stitches on all four needles, in the first round working off both legs of each double stitch as one (similar to knitting two together) when you encounter them.

After this, work the **second (bottom)** part of the heel over the stitches of the fourth and first needle only (currently on one "heel" needle).

**Row 1 (RS):** Knit across the sts of the center third and the first st of the left third, turn.

**Row 2 (WS):** Slip 1 st with yarn in front and pull out a double stitch, purl the sts of the center third and the first st of the right third, turn.

**Row 3 (RS):** Slip 1 st with yarn in front and pull out a double stitch, knit all sts, including the double stitch (through both legs), plus 1 st more, turn.

**Row 4 (WS):** Slip 1 st with yarn in front and pull out a double stitch, purl all sts, including the double stitch (through both legs), plus 1 st more, turn.

Repeat Rows 3 and 4 until both outer sts sit on the needle as double stitches.

Evenly distribute the heel stitches back onto 2 DPNs, and begin working in the round again, knitting both legs of the double stitches as one.

TIP: In this heel type, small holes may form between the first and second and the third and fourth needle. This happens because the working yarn between the heel stitches and the first or last stitch of the upper foot is not as taut as it should be. Such holes can be avoided with a little trick. After the first part of the heel, when working 2 rounds in stockinette stitch over the sts of all 4 needles, work as follows: After having knit the stitches of the first needle, place a stitch marker, and work the first two stitches of the second needle still with the same needle. Work the sts of the second needle as usual. Now, work the sts of the third needle, except for the last 2 sts. Slip these 2 sts onto the fourth needle. Work the sts of the fourth needle, and place a stitch marker after the two additional sts. Work the second half of the heel according to instructions, but work the two additional sts before and after the stitch marker not as double stitch.

    After completing the heel section, leave the additional sts on the first/fourth needle for a few more rounds, then slip them back again to their respective needles.

## STRANDED PATTERN (4-PLY FINGERING WEIGHT, YARDAGE 230 YD. / 1.75 OZ. [210 M / 50 G])

| Size | W5½/6 | W7/8 | W9/9½, M7/7½ | W11/12, M8½/9 | M10/11 | M12/13 |
|---|---|---|---|---|---|---|
| stitch count total/per needle | 64/16 | 64/16 | 68/17 | 68/17 | 72/18 | 76/19 |
| heel width, # of sts on Ndls #4 and #1 | 32 | 32 | 34 | 34 | 36 | 38 |
| heel stitch distribution | 10/12/10 | 10/12/10 | 11/12/11 | 11/12/11 | 12/12/12 | 12/14/12 |

## KNIT-PURL PATTERNS, STRIPES, ETC. (4-PLY FINGERING WEIGHT, YARDAGE 230 YD. / 1.75 OZ. [210 M / 50 G])

| Size | W5½/6 | W7/8 | W9/9½, M7/7½ | W11/12, M8½/9 | M10/11 | M12/13 |
|---|---|---|---|---|---|---|
| stitch count total/per needle | 60/15 | 60/15 | 64/16 | 64/16 | 68/17 | 72/18 |
| heel width, # of sts on Ndls #4 and #1 | 30 | 30 | 32 | 32 | 34 | 36 |
| heel stitch distribution | 10/10/10 | 10/10/10 | 10/12/10 | 10/12/10 | 11/12/11 | 12/12/12 |

## SCHOPPEL ALB LINO OR OTHER SIMILAR WEIGHT YARN (YARDAGE 437.5 YD. / 3.5 OZ. [400 M / 100 G])

| Size | W5½/6 | W7/8 | W9/9½, M7/7½ | W11/12, M8½/9 | M10/11 | M12/13 |
|---|---|---|---|---|---|---|
| Stitch count total/per needle | 56/14 | 56/14 | 60/15 | 60/15 | 64/16 | 68/17 |
| Heel width, # of sts on Ndls 4 and 1 | 28 | 28 | 30 | 30 | 32 | 34 |
| Heel stitch distribution | 9/10/9 | 9/10/9 | 10/10/10 | 10/10/10 | 10/12/10 | 11/12/11 |

## TURNED HEEL WITH HEEL FLAP

For a turned heel with heel flap, work in stockinette stitch over the stitches of the fourth and first needle only. For this, combine all stitches onto one needle. The first and last three stitches are selvage sts and are always knitted. Row 1 starts at the beginning of the round between the fourth and first needle.

### HEEL FLAP

**Row 1 (RS):** Knit all sts, turn.

**Row 2 (WS):** K3, p to last 3 sts of row, k3, turn.

Repeat Rows 1 and 2 until desired height has been reached (see tables on page 188), then start decreases. Divide the sts into 3 parts, using stitch markers between sections if needed (see tables on page 188).

Work the heel flap in stockinette stitch over the stitches of the middle section.

**Row 1 (RS):** Knit the sts of the middle section, knitting the last st of the center section together with the first st of the side part, turn.

**Row 2 (WS):** Slip the first st purlwise, purl the sts of the center section, and purl the last st of the center section together with the first st of the side part, turn.

**Row 3 (RS):** Slip the first st knitwise, knit the sts of the center section, and knit the last st together with the first st of the side part, turn.

Repeat Rows 2 and 3, until only the sts of the center section remain on the needle. Now, knit the first half of the center section sts.

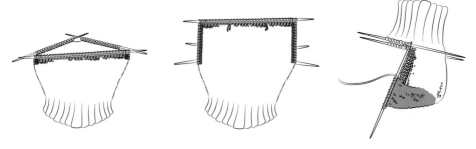

## PICKING UP STITCHES

Continue in stockinette stitch in the round. In Round 1, first knit the second half of the stitches in the center section, then pick up and knit 1 stitch each from every selvage stitch of the heel flap. For this, insert the needle from the front to the back into the selvage stitch, then pull the working yarn through as if to form a knit stitch. This way, pick up 1 stitch each from every selvage stitch in the first half of the heel flap. Now, work the stitches of the second and third needle in the charted pattern, then, using a spare DPN, pick up and knit the stitches from the second half of the heel flap as described. To finish up Round 1, now knit the stitches from the first half of the center section.

## GUSSET DECREASES

After the heel, you have more stitches on the needles than before; these extra stitches now need to be gradually decreased again. Decreases are worked in every other round on the first and fourth needle, and are repeated until the original stitch count has been reached again.

On decrease rounds knit the first needle to the last 3 stitches, knit together the third-to-last and second-to-last stitch (right-leaning decrease), knit the last stitch. On the fourth needle, knit the first stitch, slip 1 knitwise, knit the next stitch, and pass the slipped stitch over (left-leaning decrease).

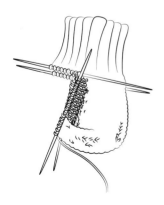

## STRANDED PATTERN (4-PLY FINGERING WEIGHT, YARDAGE 230 YD. / 1.75 OZ. [210 M / 50 G])

| Size | W5½/6 | W7/8 | W9/9½, M7/7½ | W11/12, M8½/9 | M10/11 | M12/13 |
|---|---|---|---|---|---|---|
| Stitch count total/per needle | 64/16 | 64/16 | 68/17 | 68/17 | 72/18 | 76/19 |
| Heel width # of sts on Ndls 4 and 1 | 32 | 32 | 34 | 34 | 36 | 38 |
| Heel stitch distribution | 10/12/10 | 10/12/10 | 11/12/11 | 11/12/11 | 12/12/12 | 12/14/12 |
| # of rows in heel flap | 30 | 30 | 32 | 32 | 34 | 36 |
| # of sts to pick up on each side | 15 | 15 | 16 | 16 | 17 | 18 |

## KNIT-PURL PATTERNS, STRIPES, ETC. (4-PLY FINGERING WEIGHT, YARDAGE 230 YD. / 1.75 OZ. [210 M / 50 G])

| Size | W5½/6 | W7/8 | W9/9½, M7/7½ | W11/12, M8½/9 | M10/11 | M12/13 |
|---|---|---|---|---|---|---|
| Stitch count total/per needle | 60/15 | 60/15 | 64/16 | 64/16 | 68/17 | 72/18 |
| Heel width # of sts on Ndls 4 and 1 | 30 | 30 | 32 | 32 | 34 | 36 |
| Heel stitch distribution | 10/10/10 | 10/10/10 | 10/12/10 | 10/12/10 | 11/12/11 | 12/12/12 |
| # of rows in heel flap | 28 | 28 | 30 | 30 | 32 | 34 |
| # of sts to pick up on each side | 14 | 14 | 15 | 15 | 16 | 17 |

## SCHOPPEL ALB LINO OR ANY SIMILAR WEIGHT YARN (YARDAGE 437.5 YD. M / 3.5 OZ. [400 M / 100 G])

| Size | W5½/6 | W7/8 | W9/9½, M7/7½ | W11/12, M8½/9 | M10/11 | M12/13 |
|---|---|---|---|---|---|---|
| Stitch count total/per needle | 56/14 | 56/14 | 60/15 | 60/15 | 64/16 | 68/17 |
| Heel width # of sts on Ndls 4 and 1 | 28 | 28 | 30 | 30 | 32 | 34 |
| Heel stitch distribution | 9/10/9 | 9/10/9 | 10/10/10 | 10/10/10 | 10/12/10 | 11/12/11 |
| # of rows in heel flap | 24 | 24 | 26 | 26 | 28 | 30 |
| # of sts to pick up on each side | 12 | 12 | 13 | 13 | 14 | 15 |

# TOE

## TOE WITH PAIRED BANDED DECREASES

In Round 1, on the first and third needle, knit together the third-to-last and second-to-last stitch (right-leaning decrease), and on the second and fourth needle, slip the second stitch, knit the next stitch, and pass the slipped stitch over (left-leaning decrease). Work the next 2 rounds even in stockinette stitch without decreases. Repeat decreases in Rounds 4, 6, and 8, then work decreases in every round, until only 2 stitches remain on each needle (8 stitches total). Break the working yarn, thread the end into a tapestry needle and through the remaining 8 stitches, and cinch the stitches tightly. Now, thread the end through to the wrong side, and weave it in.

## ROUNDED TOE

In Round 1, knit together the third-to-last and second-to-last stitch on the first and third needle (right-leaning decrease), and on the second and fourth needle, slip the second stitch, knit the next stitch, and pass the slipped stitch over (left-leaning decrease). Work the next 2 rounds even in stockinette stitch without decreases. Repeat decreases in Rounds 4, 6, and 8, then work decreases in every round, until for shoe sizes Women's 5½ to Women's 9½/ Men's 7½, only 5 stitches remain on each needle, and for shoe sizes Women's 11/Men's 8½ to Men's 11, 6 stitches. Graft the remaining opening in Kitchener stitch (see page 190), and hide the end.

# KITCHENER GRAFTING

Combine the stitches of the first and fourth needle on one DPN, and the stitches of the second and third needle on another. Both needles have to bear the same number of stitches. Place both DPNs on top of each other; break the working yarn, leaving a long tail for grafting; thread it into a dull tapestry needle; and start grafting at the right edge of the piece.

**1.** Insert the tapestry needle purlwise into the first stitch of the front DPN, and pull the yarn through. Leave the stitch on the DPN.

**2.** Now, lead the tapestry needle through the first stitch of the back DPN knitwise, and pull the yarn through. Leave this stitch on the DPN too.

**3.** Lead the tapestry needle knitwise through the first stitch of the front DPN, and slip the stitch off of the DPN. Now, lead the tapestry needle purlwise through the next stitch, pull the yarn through, and leave the stitch on the DPN.

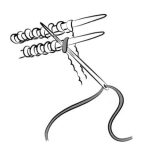

## ABBREVIATIONS

DPN(s) = double-pointed needle(s)
k = knit
Ndl(s) = needle(s), DPN
p = purl
rep = repeat
rnd(s) = round(s)
RS = right side
st(s) = stitch(es)
St st = stockinette stitch
tbl = through the back loop
WS = wrong side
yo = yarn over

**4.** Lead the tapestry needle purlwise through the first stitch of the back DPN, pull the yarn through, and slip the stitch off of the DPN. Now, lead the tapestry needle through the next stitch of the back DPN knitwise. Pull the yarn through, and leave the stitch on the DPN.

Repeat Steps 3 and 4 until all stitches have been grafted. Finish off by threading the tail through to the wrong side and weaving it in.

**Kerstin Balke** learned knitting at the age of six from her grandmother. She has made pullovers, jackets, scarves, hats, and even fine tablecloths over the years, but her true passion is the knitted sock. For several years she has been designing her own patterns under the name Stine & Stitch. She lives with her husband and her two daughters between Hamburg and Lübeck, Germany.

# ACKNOWLEDGMENTS

Thank you to my family, for enduring my never-ending chatter about socks, colors, and patterns, and putting up with WIP clutter all over the place, with virtually no complaints.

To my test knitters, whose works can be admired on Instagram, for their speedy execution of my instructions, and the wonderful feedback. Without your diligence, numerous mistakes would have been able to sneak in! Thanks Andrea (@natuerlichkreativ), Barbara (@thoni_knits), Betina (@nordfrau), Claudia (@reetselig), Etha, Isa (@luisa_wolkenschein), Kirsten (@knightly-art), Konstanze (@lilliliebtlollis), Lydia (@lydiafisch), Marianne (@runningyarn), Sabine (@hexbexhamburg), Steffi (@lille_boat), and Svenja (@foerdefaden).

# TECHNIQUE INDEX

back loop, working through, 172

cast-on, long tail, 168
charts, how to read, 182
cuff, how to work, 178

decreases: knitting 2 stitches together, 173; slip-knit-pass; 173; slip-slip-knit, 173

gauge, 177
gusset, 187

heel, boomerang, 183
heel, turned with heel flap, 185

Kitchener grafting, 190
knit stitch, 170

leg, how to work, 179

needles, knitting, 166
notions, 167

picking up stitches, 187
purl stitch, 171

short rows, German, with double stitch, 172
sizing, 176
stranded colorwork, how to work, 180

toe, paired banded decreases, 189
toe, rounded, 189

yarn, 166
yarn over, 173